CHILDREN IN THE WAY

New directions for the Church's children

A Report from the General Synod Board of Education

National Society

Church House Publishing

ISBN 0 7151 4766 8

Published January 1988 for the General Synod Board of Education jointly by The National Society and Church House Publishing, Church House, Great Smith Street, London SW1P 3NZ

Fifth impression October 1989

Printed in England by Tasprint

CHILDREN
IN THE WAY

Contents

Acknowledgements

We wish to record our thanks to all those who contributed to the work and thinking in this Report. In particular we thank

the Diocesan Advisers who administered the survey and who contributed ideas and examples;

the parishes who completed the Questionnaires;

the College Trusts who provided funds for the Survey:

All Saints Educational Trust,
the Foundation of St Matthias,
the Hockerill Educational Foundation,
St Gabriel's Trust,
the Sarum St Michael Educational Charity,
St Christopher's Trust,

and the Central Church Fund of the Church of England;

St Christopher's College Association who provided additional information;

the children who contributed their thinking, especially the children of Hope-under-Dinmore and Goodrich schools, the children of St Catherine's Church, Gloucester and the congregation of St Mark's, Coulby Newham;

The Revd Gillian Muddiman who wrote the theological reflection in chapter 6;

The Revd Dr Leslie Francis and Mr David Lankshear, who wrote the report of the Survey in chapter 7;

Canon Roger Grey, who met with the Working Party and gave valuable advice;

our secretaries who struggled with the typing and revisions.

REPORT WORKING PARTY

Miss Margaret Turk (chairperson)
The Revd Carole Copland (until October 1986), diocesan Adviser York Diocese
Mr Richard O Hughes, Director of Education Salisbury Diocese
Mrs Dorothy Jamal, diocesan Adviser Bristol Diocese
Mr Steve Pearce, diocesan Adviser Derby Diocese
Miss Marjorie Freeman, Children's Officer, Board of Education.

Preface
by The Bishop of London

Recently the responsibility of society for children has come much to the fore. Part of this thrust has arisen from concern about their physical safety, partly it has come about because of changing views about the place of children in the community, and partly because they have become targets for advertising pressure. The 'world' of children has changed radically in the last ten years, with new opportunities as well as fresh restrictions and new pressures from society.

It is therefore an opportune time for the Church to re-examine its own responsibilities towards the children with whom it is in contact, and towards those outside its direct influence. This Report has been written with all these issues in mind. It uses information gathered from a survey conducted in twenty-five dioceses of the Church of England to examine the present situation. It goes on to look at models for Christian education, and to suggest interesting and challenging ways for the Church to go forward in integrating children fully into the life of the Church.

Consequently, this is an important Report for the whole Church to consider, and I strongly commend it not only to the attention of the General Synod but also to those concerned with the care of children in and by the Church.

✝ Graham London:

Introduction

'The Church that does not accept children unconditionally in its fellowship is depriving those children of what is rightfully theirs, but the deprivation such as the Church itself will suffer is far more grave.'
(*The Child in the Church* Report)

Imagine a Church congregation in which men and women, girls and boys, young and old, share together to worship God, to learn from one another about their faith, to pray together about their mutual concerns and joys, to serve those in need and to reach out with the Gospel to those in the community who are outside the Church. Whenever possible, the members are not separated into groups according to age or sex but are together. At times, of course, there *are* activities for parents and very young children, a club for lively junior age children, a group for adolescents and study sessions for adults. But the first instinct of this Church is to say 'What can we *all* do?' This is the vision of the authors of this report. Although we recognise that there may be many steps along the way before some parishes can achieve the reality, we ask you to share in this vision.

The concern of this Report is to look at the place of children in the Church. This means challenging those who make decisions and those who work with children's groups. We want them to acknowledge once more the responsibility which all adults have to share their faith with the children of the Church and to go out to children and families outside the Church. We believe that this is to be accomplished by developing relationships between people of all ages within the Church, and between Church people and children and families outside the Church. We are therefore more concerned with sharing our journey of faith with children than with pursuing 'traditional' patterns of Sunday school teaching in any formal sense. The double meaning in

1

our title is quite deliberate. We want children to come 'into the way of faith' with adults. We want adults to overcome any feelings that children are merely 'in the way'. So often the Church may appear to be indifferent to the needs of children and, sadly, some adults are unaware of the contribution which children can make to the life of the Church.

Now seems to be a particularly appropriate time to reconsider the place of children in the Church. It is twelve years since the report *The Child in the Church* was published and eleven years since it was debated briefly in General Synod. Since then there have been many changes in the lives and attitudes of children themselves. It is therefore time to reappraise the position and to question whether a new situation and new attitudes demand a new approach to children's work by the Church.

This Report is addressed to General Synod, but also to members of diocesan and deanery Synods, PCCs, diocesan, deanery and parish education committees and leaders of children's groups. The ideas within it arise from the experience and study of those who advise on children's work in dioceses and parishes and those who are involved in children's groups, as well as from the insights of children themselves. It is rooted in the reality of good practice.

From the first, however, it was recognised that informed debate on the place of children in the Church should involve a clear assessment of current practice and provision. Recommendations for future policy and action need to be anchored in a realistic appreciation of the contemporary starting points. With this in mind, the working party stimulated the formation of a research project running parallel to and inter-acting with its own deliberations. Based on twenty-five dioceses of the Church of England, it registers both the scale of the task and the substantial contribution the Church of England is already making.

Some definition of childhood is necessary, and for the purpose of the Survey and Report it was decided to include people from birth to thirteen years. The earliest years are of the greatest importance in the formation of attitudes and the laying of foundations of belief and understanding. We therefore begin with the baby and the family. We assume that by thirteen years most youngsters have reached puberty and will consider themselves as young people or young adults. So we have decided to end our consideration of children at thirteen years. But in our thinking, age differences are less important than a shared Christian calling to walk in the way of Christ. For us children are

2

important; people with needs to be met and a contribution to make to the life of the Church. This view may not be shared by all Church members or Church congregations. Some accept and welcome the children in their own right, some are merely tolerant, some are sentimental in their attitude towards them and some see children as of no importance.

In the Report we look at the position of children in society today and at styles of outreach and mission. We then examine models for Christian education work. This leads us to reflect on the way in which faith grows and on ways of providing the environment for that growth, and to look at the practical implications for leaders. The theological thinking and assumptions of the working party will be apparent throughout the Report, but it was thought to be important to invite a theologian to look at it with a fresh mind and to draw together some of the Biblical ideas and concepts discernible in it. Finally, an account of the results of the survey is given.

Our conviction is simple. If children are to continue in the way of faith, if they are to continue on the path to which the Church welcomed them at baptism, then they must be aided and supported by the adult fellow-Christians who are also on that journey and must be acknowledged as those who sometimes lead the way. We invite you to join us in searching for new strategies and models for Christian education in parishes, in order that both adults and children may journey together in the way of Christ, growing into his full stature and serving his world.

1. Childhood Today

CHILDHOOD

'Dear adults I like writing letters but this is a special one. It's about being a little girl. I absolutely hate it. It's just like a sock when it falls down, you get pulled right up again. You always get told what to do and what not to do. I can't wait to grow up to be an adult. Love Zoey. 11 years.' (from *Dear Adults*)

'When you're a child you always want to be an adult and when you're an adult you would like to start again.' (13 years. From *Dear Adults*)

1.1   The child's world is changing and the place of the child in the world is changing. For that reason alone it seemed necessary to reconsider the place of children in our Church, and the responsibility of the Church to put children in the way of faith.

1.2   During the twentieth century increasing attention has been paid to the notion of childhood and adolescence. The work of educational and developmental psychologists, beginning with the research of Jean Piaget (1896-1980), has made us sharply aware of the importance of the experiences of infants and children. Although their work may not be universally accepted, their influence on educational practice and the understanding of infancy and childhood is clearly discernible. Children have been taken seriously in their own right. The intellectual ability of a small child, for example, has been valued at its own level: different in nature from that of the mature adult, appropriate for the child and a necessary and important stage in his or her progression to mature, rational thinking. We have also learned to appreciate the child's ideas and intuitive understanding, and to take them seriously.

We need to accept the idea that a child's knowledge of God and understanding of faith must also be valued at its own level and for the

4

child's own sake. The research of the Religious Experience Research Unit at Oxford threw up many examples of spiritual experience and religious insight which belonged to the young child.

> 'I remember sitting in my mother's lap at the age of five while she affectionately explained the idea of God as a very nice and poetic way of explaining things but just like a fairy tale. I felt embarrassed at what seemed abysmal blindness and ignorance and felt sorry for her'

said one woman who was interviewed. (*The Original Vision*, E Robinson. RERU)

1.3　It is now twelve years since *The Child in the Church* Report was published by the Consultative Group for Ministry among Children. It was, and continues to be, a seminal document for anyone concerned with the Christian nurture of children. Indeed, a further report, *Understanding Christian Nurture*, was added to it in 1981. Many changes have occurred in society since 1976, and the 1980s and 1990s bring their own opportunities and problems. The following picture of the life of children today has been drawn from the experience of many Diocesan Advisers working with children, together with evidence taken from official reports and other publications concerned with children in society at the present time.

CHILDREN'S CHOICES

> *'I saw a great toy on television, but when I got it, it was rubbish!'*

1.4　The child has, in many ways, become the centre of attention in our society today. The commercial world bombards quite small children with television advertisements for toys, for example; the promotion of children's fashions in clothes encourages the child to choose what he or she wants and to make those desires clear. Indeed, most children make their own decisions about what to wear and, within some limits, about what to do. Many have their own television sets and access to video recorders, so they choose their own programmes to watch. In formal education too they are encouraged to make choices about activities and projects, to make discoveries and to find out information for themselves. The child, then, has perhaps greater freedom of choice than at any time in our history; this puts a greater responsibility and power in his or her hands.

The child is less of a conformist than in the past. He or she is much more likely to say 'I think... I want... why should I?' There are obviously some inferences here for Christian nurture and the style of our Christian education work. Children need some secure framework in which to learn and grow. They need to know where they stand. They need freedom to explore and discover. They need the opportunity to challenge the ideas of other people and to share their understandings of God and his world.

1.5 For many children today life is full of opportunity. Although not as widely available as they might be, facilities to pursue creative activities or physical skills are in fact more widespread than ever before. Children on the whole are encouraged to develop their interests to the full – but we need to bear in mind the many consequent demands on the time of some children. The width of the range of choices of activity available to them can itself be a difficulty. In some families, timetables for evenings and weekends revolve almost entirely around the activities of the children, who have to be taken to and collected from their classes and groups.

Parishes where families are in this kind of situation need to assess carefully the demands which they make on the busy lives of both children and parents. The Church has many rivals for the children's interest and time, and probably only relates to those who come to Sunday school, or to a group, for less than one per cent of their time. The quality of what we offer the children is therefore important also and not least the quality of relationships which is available to them.

1.6 At the other end of the scale are the children who have few interests and those whose parents have little or no interest in their activities. Many children state that TV is their main leisure activity. A Playboard enquiry showed that for every child who chose organised activities, three preferred non-organised leisure time (*Make Way* for *Children's Play*, Playboard, 1985.) These are the youngsters who have little desire to join in any organised activity and yet who are bored. They are likely to alleviate their boredom by vandalism and even petty crime. In 1985, 53,000 children between 10 and 13 were found guilty of offences and given formal police warnings, and 11,500 were found guilty of offences by the Courts (*Criminal Statistics*, 1985).

The availability of cigarettes, alcohol and drugs is also a grave matter of concern. Youngsters who are looking for anaesthetics from a world which they find difficult and purposeless find them here. This is true of children from all kinds of backgrounds; the child who appears to be in no way disadvantaged may well get caught into this

6

scene. The importance of peer pressure in this, as in other matters, must not be underestimated; the same children who will be idealistic about the needs of the Third World may also be involved in local vandalism and may see no connection between the two situations.

'The worst thing about being young is the thought of unemployment' (13 year old).

1.7   A *Guardian* survey into the concerns of young people aged from 10 to 17 reported that the thought of unemployment is the most widely-felt national problem today, followed by the issue of nuclear weapons and war, and then by crime and violence. But around a quarter of those interviewed said that nothing much concerned them at all (*The Guardian*, 7.1.87). Is the Church saying or doing enough about this disease in society, about - for example - the lack of purpose induced by unemployment and the prospect for children of unemployment? Should we be making some contribution to thinking about education for life - which may or may not include paid employment - and examining our Church school and Church-based teaching to see how far it is helping to provide this? Should we not be looking for imaginative ways of reaching unattached children?

PRESSURES OF SOCIETY

A five-year-old was told of the death of his grandfather.
'Who shot him?' was the instant reply.

1.8   The growth of freedom of choice for children has taken place at a time when there is a more authoritative style of government, and yet society as a whole is challenging many aspects of authority, and wrestling with problems of law and order. The authority of the police and the law, for example, is challenged constantly, and is seen by children and adults to be challenged when they watch television news. Violence as an expression of frustration, as well as lawlessness, can be seen daily in media coverage of home and global situations. Children cannot fail to be influenced by the attitudes which these events disclose.

1.9   The influence of television and videos is a complex issue. Available evidence points to many beneficial results as well as some disturbing ones. The essays in the report *Parents Talking Television* (Comedia) mostly emphasise the pleasures and possibilities of television in the family.

It says, for example,

'Television can be a doorway opening on those areas of human experience which anxiety, embarrassment or plain ignorance sometimes close us off from sharing.'

On the other hand, the report of the informal working party of parliamentarians and churchmen, *Video, Violence and Children,* draws attention to new elements in the portrayal of violence in many films which are seen by children. The values and assumptions underlying the portrayal of violence in folk-tales and children's stories ensured that the perpetrator of violence was never the hero, and good always triumphed over evil. This is not true of many videos; indeed, the viewer is invited to enter into the drama from the standpoint of the perpetrator of the violence. The greatest danger consequent on this approach, as on the general portrayal of violence on television, is to those who already have a tendency to aggression and to children who lack wise parental support and a safe home environment. We must not, however, ignore the insidious way in which Christian values in society can be undermined as a whole, and the effect of this on children.

'To make Church more interesting for me I would like to
watch 5 cartoons on a television hanging on the ceiling.'

1.10 Despite the excellence of some religious broadcasting and television, the programmes most likely to be heard or seen by children give a very strange view of religion and the Church. State religious occasions, ineffectual or 'dotty' vicars in comedy series, a sincere but somewhat fanatically religious woman in a soap opera: these are the likely diet, and they do little to show the essential involvement of faith with people's lives. However, the authority of the Church and of the Bible are themselves called to question at the present time and we cannot blame popular television for largely ignoring an aspect of life which is apparently of no importance to most people.

1.11 Also through the influence of the media and from attitudes in society generally, children today have acquired a sexual awareness which is more developed than was the case in the childhood of older generations. An openness about sexual matters in society means that children have imbibed knowledge and attitudes which can be difficult for them to handle. The 'page three' approach is seen by many boys and girls to be the norm, as is, regrettably, the expectation of sexual

8

experience at an early age. The Church, and Christian parents in particular, have a difficult task in presenting ideals of good, loving relationships and in encouraging a reverence for life and for respect of other people which is at the heart of moral sexual behaviour. In an interview with Bernard Levin in *The Times* (March 30, 1987), the Archbishop of Canterbury says that the moral energy which is needed in present society will be found by

> 'giving us a sense that life is worthwhile, by recovering some sense of wonder, recovering some sense that we have a purpose in being here... What gives me the vision I need for my choices, the moral energy I need to face up to my responsibilities is God... If we are to have a free society which is essential if love, not power is going to rule the world then we can't have some people – people who believe in God – in a position to tell other people what they should believe and how they should behave. Of course, it is difficult for the growing child to know what to do or to know how to behave; because there are many, many more options open nowadays. It is a matter of guiding and teaching, not commanding and ordering. It depends on getting the better things taught; truth, longsuffering, gentleness, tolerance and the fruits of the spirit.'

There are tasks here for the Church to influence society in an acceptable but challenging way and to assist parents to work out their stances on this matter.

> '*I was abused myself from the age of four. I was a neurotic, nervous child with a terrible sense of fear, though I did not realise fully what had happened until I was a teenager.*' (Worker at Incest Crisis Line.)

1.12   Adults do need to be aware of the dangers which may confront children in their families and within their care. Child neglect and child abuse, of which we are presently aware, is a scandal about which none can be complacent. In 1986 the NSPCC register showed an increase of 34 per cent of cases of child abuse over the figures for 1985. More than half of these were cases of physical abuse, 31.5 per cent were of sexual abuse, 7.4 per cent were cases of neglect, and 2.5 per cent were cases of emotional abuse. It is estimated that at least 1 in 10 adults was sexually abused as a child. In June 1987 the NSPCC said that cases of abuse continue to double each year. Exact figures are difficult to establish, but Finkelhor's study (1979-80) indicates that 19 per cent of women and 9 per cent of men have been sexually assaulted, and other studies suggest higher numbers (cf. *Child Abuse, the Educational Perspective,* edited by Peter Maher (Blackwell).) A greater awareness of abuse largely accounts for the increase in cases being reported. A concern to protect both children and those accused of assaulting them presents many problems both to the public and to professional workers and officials. Many schools have undertaken a programme of education to alert children to dangers, to teach them how to cope with potentially harmful situations and to be on the alert for possible problems. So too have some of the uniformed and other organisations.

Churches also must not be too complacent. Child abuse occurs in all strata of society and in all kinds of situations. The parish needs to be aware of dangers, and to be ready to cope both with victims and assailants. Leaders of children's groups need to be selected with great care, for both children and leaders need to be safeguarded. As legislation regarding disclosure of criminal records of crimes against children has been tightened up, there is even greater need for those responsible for appointing unpaid leaders of children's groups to be wary. They must ensure that they do not appoint people who have been, or would be, unacceptable as leaders.

1.13   Because of potential dangers, many children today are denied the physical freedom to come and go alone to their different activities. This is at variance with the freedom of choice described above; as a result their activities may be curtailed and they may lose some independence and opportunity for adventure with their peers. There may be a need in some areas for the provision of supervised adventure opportunities.

FAMILY LIFE

'I thought how like bereavement a divorce can be. I was on my own with Caroline (aged three)... when we separated, her daddy visiting about every third Saturday. When one week he had again not showed up she was upset and said, "Daddies don't do that, I'm not calling him Daddy."' (From Children under Pressure, *Pat Wynnejones (Triangle).)*

1.14   A further change in the lives of children today must be noted, and that is the shape of family life. It is calculated that around five per cent of all families in Great Britain are one-parent families with dependent children (*Social Trends*, 1987 edition, HMSO). More than one in ten of all dependent children live in one-parent families headed by the mother.

The fact that more single women keep their babies today, and the numbers of marriage separations and divorces account for these figures. The number of decrees absolute granted in 1985 was 175,000, an increase of 11 per cent on 1984 and more than double the figure for 1971. The annual numbers of divorcees remarrying doubled between 1971 and 1985 (*Population Trends 45*, HMSO). The Church itself increasingly has in its congregations one-parent families and divorced and remarried people while the incidence of marriage breakdown in clergy families is now proportionately the same as for the rest of the population.

1.15   Children in our churches, as elsewhere, are coping with marriage break-up and separation. Many of them feel guilty when one parent leaves the family, imagining that something they have done has caused the parent to decide to go. The financial stringencies which sometimes follow these events also cause confusion and anxiety in some children. It must be stressed, however, that many one-parent families are good secure families, and that some children are happier when a situation of conflict is resolved. Increasingly, however, children have to face the re-adjustment to new families on the remarriage of one or both parents, sharing one parent with a new partner and children, or visiting a parent who is apparently absorbed in a new spouse and another family of children. Some children are amazingly resilient and adaptable to these circumstances, whilst others exhibit symptoms of distress and disturbance either at the time or later on.

1.16   There are therefore questions which the local church may need to ask itself. We must not delude ourselves that these situations exist only outside the Church. There will be children and parents needing our support within our congregations and groups. Are there particular needs of single parents to be met in the church and in the neighbourhood? How aware do leaders need to be of the stresses and strains for children in their groups during a time of marriage breakup? Is there a need for comfortable surroundings where a parent could take a child for regular access visits? How is any single person made to feel part of the Church 'family'?

1.17   The Church as a whole also needs to address itself to questions like the model of Christian family life and commitment which should realistically be presented to children and young people when divorce and remarriage may be seen to be the norm. The actuality is that the majority of marriages survive. What is the place of Christian teaching on forgiveness and reconciliation in all this? It is not only a matter of what is said, but of the hidden messages that are given by an illustration, a tone of voice or an underlying assumption. What model of the Church is appropriate if the scriptural model of a family headed by the father is no longer experienced by some of its children? What do we say about God as Father? It now seems clear that many children with an absent or 'bad' father build up for themselves a picture of an ideal father, but we need to be sensitive to their situations, and realistic in our approaches.

CHILDREN IN THE WAY

1.18   There is a sense in which the helplessness of small children will arouse feelings of protectiveness and nostalgia among adults. Deep down there is often, too, a jealousy of the years ahead of them and the opportunities open to them. Perhaps at the present time there should also be a greater awareness of the gulf between children and adults. Adults see the range of activities offered to children and are surprised at their apathy and boredom. How can they say so often, 'I don't care', 'It doesn't matter'? Though our minds may present some explanations – the age they're at, the feelings of futility about employment, the future of the world and so on – our imaginations are not able to take on board the way these affect their lives and outlook. For example:

> 'How can I, as an adult, know what it feels like to be a child who has no image, and therefore no ambition, about what I want to be when I grow up?'

The rapid technological advances of this age have also left many adults behind. To see a five-year-old confidently using a computer which to an adult may still be a complicated mystery, to appreciate the matter-of-factness with which most children treat the possibilities of space travel when for many adults it still savours of science fiction, is to begin to realise the gulf between adults and children. In Church life and in our attempts to reach out to children outside the Church, we must be aware of this gulf. It is certainly as great as, if not greater than at any time in history. One thing we can do is to listen to the children themselves; to try to learn from them what their lives are like; to enter into their deeper feelings about their present and their future.

1.19   The Church will fail the children and their families if it does not take such account of the lives which they lead. The educational task of the Church (as we shall discuss more fully in chapters 3 and 4) includes helping its members of all ages to grow in relationship with God and with each other, and to find meaning and purpose in their own lives and in the world around them. To do this it needs to share with them the Christian story from the past, help them to discover their hopes for the future, and engage with their present experiences.

1.20 The Church also has a responsibility to those outside its worshipping members. There are issues to be raised with society at large on behalf of children and families, and there are children to be helped. There are more children outside the Church than within it, and we have a responsibility to reach out to them with the Gospel.

To achieve our purposes we need to meet the children in the context of the society in which they are growing and learning and acquiring attitudes, and share with them the discovery of their faith, a faith which seems relevant to them for the life which they have to live.

RECOMMENDATIONS

1   The Church should seriously consider what priority it places on serving the needs of all children in our contemporary society. Parishes, deaneries and dioceses should acknowledge their responsibility

— to learn from those already involved in social work with children,
— to investigate particular local pressures on children,
— to establish practical ways of contributing to children's support and enrichment.

2   PCCs should carefully consider the suitability of new leaders to whom they delegate responsibility for work with children in the parish.

2. Children on the Edge

EVANGELISM

'I don't know why people out of the goodness of their hearts bother holding services because very little people come.' (Nine-year-old)

2.1   This nine-year-old has a somewhat jaundiced view of churchgoing, despite a compassionate feeling for those who arrange church services! Our Survey, however, shows that we do not need to be as despondent as he is. Some 400,000 children are regularly involved in Sunday school and similar activities in the Church of England, and, for example, 343,000 are in contact with the Church through uniformed organisations. This does not mean that we can be complacent. For some children the links may be fairly tenuous, and there are many children and parents outside the reach of any church. We therefore need to discover appropriate methods of mission and outreach if these children too are to be brought into the way of faith.

2.2   Our first problem may lie in our own hesitancy. How appropriate is a policy of evangelisation of children? Have we the necessary resources, or time? How shall we make contact? In an article in the *Tablet* (March 14, 1987), John Wyngaards says:

'Evangelisation means selling a parcel of ready-made truths, we think, or persuading people to accept a new moral code. This is a narrow and distorted view. In Luke's gospel Jesus tells us: "You shall be my witness" (Luke 24.48). This has to be taken in an existential sense. We are to testify not to some doctrinal truths, but to the new life Jesus gives us; to the meaningful way we can relate to ourselves, to others and to God, through Jesus. Evangelisation means communicating to trusted friends our personal religious experience, our conviction and our commitment.

There is no room here for coercion, hard sell or manipulation. Rather, we reach out in a way that respects otherness and individual response.'

Here perhaps are some clues to our approach towards reaching children and families on the edge of the Church and outside it, and putting them in the way of Christ. We need to meet them where they are, and to build up our relationships with them.

2.3   We will first look then at ways in which parishes have reached, or could reach, those outside the Church, then look at ways of building on contacts already in existence, and finally look at the Church's concern for children in society at large.

CHILDREN OUTSIDE THE CHURCH

'To be a religious person you'd have to believe in some sort of religion, strongly believe in it, not just kind of "well it might be true and it might not", you'd have to actually believe it was actually true, to be a religious person'. (Ten-year-old)

2.4   There is some evidence that, while young people generally are not convinced about the place and importance of the Church, they are searching for a faith and for spirituality. One style of reaching out to them is through direct evangelistic campaigns. Such campaigns, or missions, in a parish often contain within them programmes for the children, and some are directed principally at children and their parents. For example, the Church Army, amongst others, runs children's beach missions and also children's missions in parishes. Significantly many of the latter are now called Family Weeks; efforts are made to reach the children's parents, and to involve the adult members of the congregation in preparation and follow-up as well as in the events of the week. Usually there are separate meetings for younger and older children after school each day, visits to schools, meetings for parents and, often, a Saturday programme of activities and story for children, with a final offering of the week at the Sunday parish worship. One parish in our Survey reported that 76 two to five-year-olds, 216 six to nine-year-olds and 229 ten to thirteen-year-olds attended the evening sessions of a children's mission in the parish.

2.5   We note, too, the continuing groups for children organised by Scripture Union, Crusaders and other organisations which often meet in lunch hours in schools, and which seek to present Christianity to children as a way of life to which they can commit themselves.

2.6   Children are also included, with or without special programmes, in adult missions. In the 41 Billy Graham meetings during

'Mission England' in 1984 there was a high percentage of 'enquirers' at all meetings, and of these 9 per cent were aged 10 or under (44 per cent boys), while 18 per cent were aged 11 to 13 years (41 per cent boys). 74 per cent of those aged 10 or under and 68 per cent of those aged 11 to 13 said that they wished to accept Jesus Christ as personal Saviour, as against just under 47 per cent of adults. Proportions of those seeking assurance of salvation and of those wishing to rededicate their lives to Christ were higher among adults. (*Mission England, What Really Happened*, Philip Back (MARC Europe).) It would seem that we must not discount the desire of children to commit themselves to Christ, though we must also safeguard them from undue pressure which could lead to a superficial response, or from disproportionate feelings of guilt if they fall back from it. As we shall see in chapter 4 there are many stages on the way to mature faith, and questioning of one's own apparently secure faith is a natural, necessary process for many people.

2.7 The great need, as those who organise such campaigns recognise, is for careful follow-up. Children of highly committed families sometimes need sensitive support if they later begin to question their own commitment, and the parents need help with their own feelings of failure and guilt if the children 'fall away'. Nor is it easy for a child from an uncommitted family to take on a new way of life without the understanding and support of his or her friends and family. Every endeavour needs to be made to provide a Christian peer group to which the child can relate, as well as to reach the parents and gain their co-operation. We need to provide general support for the child, so that he or she can grow in faith and understanding in fellowship with other Christians. Perhaps our concern ought to be to convert parents or families rather than children, and to look for ongoing ways of working with family groups. Examples of such groups will be found in chapter 5.

VARIETIES OF MISSION

2.8 Every parish will have its own strengths and weaknesses with which to work, and the needs of a particular community will suggest different priorities. For some the emphasis will need to be on evangelism, on outreach to the community by the proclamation of the Gospel. For other parishes it may be more appropriate to tackle the social needs of the area, and proclaim the good news by caring action rather than by a call to commitment. One town-centre church provides a crèche where children can be safely and happily left while the adults shop; another provides a place for play or a quiet place for homework after school and before parents get home from work. Another has set up a counselling service for children and parents. In one rural area the children are collected for a 'youth club' held in one of the parishes. Yet another parish decided to establish a group for the many very young parents of newly baptised babies, to help them to think about bringing up their children as Christians. At the first meeting they discovered that what these young parents most wanted was a kind of youth club for themselves, and a baby-sitting service to enable them to attend it!

2.9   So the first concern must be to discover the needs of the area. This may involve training people to talk with and listen carefully to the opinions of those in the community and then to investigate the resources, human and financial, before deciding on any new project. The aims of the project need to be clear and the PCC needs to be committed and in agreement with what is being attempted. We need to decide how to evaluate such work. What do we count as success? It is all to easy to see it only in terms of increased (or otherwise) Church membership. It may be more important to demonstrate the Church's selfless concern and love for children by providing holidays for disadvantaged families or a drop-in club for children at a loose end, and our evaluation may be in terms of the renewed vigour of a tired parent, or the evidence of a developing trust between a child and a Church member.

2.10   The children with whom we are already in contact need to share in expressing our Christian love for others. They need to have a model of the Church which encompasses awareness of others' needs and compassion as well as of learning and worship. The happy, thriving church is often one in which this balance has been obtained, as the church shares and worships God together and expresses Christ's love to others.

2.11   We also need to remember that the Church - and Christ - is represented to children outside the Church by the attitudes and behaviour of Church members.

> 'He's supposed to be good; he goes to church, but he never notices me and almost knocked me over as he rushed to his car,'

said one small boy.

'It was not what anyone said or did but what they *were* that helped me most as a child,'

commented an adult.

CHILDREN ON THE EDGE

I was chatting to Peter, aged 8 or 9, from a non-church-going family. He explained he wouldn't be in church next week because he had to go into hospital. When we had chatted briefly about that he said nonchalantly,
'I wouldn't come next week anyway. I don't like going to Church.'
'What don't you like about it?'
'Well... they sing funny songs.'
'Yes, I suppose hymns are a bit funny sometimes! What do you think is funny about them?'
'Well, they've got bad language in them.'
(Pause) 'Bad language?'
'Yes. Things like "God almighty" and "Jesus Christ"...'

2.12   Peter's experience suggests that an introduction to Christianity through worship only can be an ambivalent experience. More often both an adult's and a child's first contact with the Church is through informal groups rather than through Sunday worship and learning activities. Where these groups are intended to be directly evangelistic in nature, the parish needs to think through carefully the requirements of membership and the method of introducing Christian learning and commitment. It is all too easy to organise a week-night group or a holiday club which attracts membership from children looking only for recreational activities, to whom its Church connections are not clear, and to whom efforts to teach or evangelise come as an unwelcome shock. Either most of the members leave, or the original intentions of the parish are lost as the demands of the members 'just to play' are met. It may well be that the needs of the community at that time are for a club without strings, and the Church might find that it has a role to play in providing it. We always need to be clear about what most urgently needs to be done.

2.13   When it seems to be appropriate to organise a children's club where the members will be given Christian education and challenge, we must set out these intentions to prospective members clearly and sensitively.

18

'This is a club run by St Blogg's Church. We play games and have exciting activities and we try to learn together about what it means to be a Christian.'

If it is hoped to bring the children into the fellowship of the Church, the stages by which this will be achieved need to be worked out. At what times will it be appropriate to meet other members of the church, share in a church service, join in a social event or a piece of service to the community? How will the support of the youngsters' parents be gained? How is the church congregation to be prepared to receive them? How far are we ready to accept the limitations of the children's circumstances?

The brothers at a club who said:

'We enjoyed making those Christian Aid posters to go in Church for Harvest. But we won't come to the service, our Dad will say we're soft'

had gone as far as they could at that time. They also had some very fresh and clear-sighted ideas about God and the practical living out of Christian beliefs.

2.14 Providing opportunities to talk about Christianity with children 'on the edge' and bringing them at least to think about Christian commitment and the way of faith is important. Its later effects may be far greater than we imagine at the time. Many children today have no concept of what it means to be a Christian, and may never have known a committed Christian person nor shared in Christian worship. The task of providing these experiences is the responsibility of the Church (including its Aided schools) and can be achieved when relationships with the young people have been built up through informal groups or family contact or uniformed organisations.

2.15   In any contacts with children 'on the edge' there is needed a very special sensitivity for those whose families are committed members of other faiths. We do children no service if we put them into an insoluble situation of divided loyalties which robs them of a sense of security and which raises the antagonism of the parents. There is much work still to be done on the appropriate Christian approach to those of other faiths; we believe it is extremely important that the particular situation of children be remembered in the development of any new policies.

2.16   Many Churches could take greater advantage of their contact with uniformed groups, particularly Church sponsored groups. We welcome initiatives like the work on spirituality of children and young people undertaken by the Scout and Guide Movements, the work of the (non-uniformed) Girls' Friendly Society, the Christian teaching of the Boys' and Girls' Brigade, the Church Lads and Church Girls' Brigade and the faithful work by chaplains to these groups. Many of their leaders look to the Church for help in implementing the 'Duty to God' and Christian education sections of their work, and in some organisations like the Boys' and Girls' Brigade, the CLB, CGB and GFS, this expectation is a matter of policy.

2.17 Our Survey showed that 20 per cent of parishes hold regular parade services. This provides an obvious point of contact with many children. Perhaps more could be done to liaise with the leaders and the young people in preparing for these services. One parish asks a different 'youth' organisation to prepare the service each month. An annual meeting of leaders discusses principles, themes and resources. The leaders consult with the parish staff or education committee members as needed, and the organisation takes full responsibility for the service on the day, asking parish staff to lead or speak if it seems appropriate. Parents support the services well, and the result is a regular act of worship which reaches out to many people on the edge of the Church at a level with which it can cope.

Building those adults and children into fuller understanding and membership depends largely on the relationships which can be developed from that starting-point. Opportunities need to be made for children to get to know regular members of the congregation. Occasional social events might be organised, or the one-off work programme in which they are asked to share. One parish has three or four days a year when the church and grounds are put in good shape by members of the congregation, all ages working together. We need to guard against feelings of exploitation, of course, but a personal request to help might provide a very natural way of building relationships with the Church.

2.18 We need to be aware that neither children nor adults may know the Christian story. Many adults feel embarrassed at their lack of knowledge and experience of religion and the Church. Parents might be helped over the first hurdle by an invitation to join a short-term enquirers' group where some basic information is imparted with opportunity for questions. This will avoid any feeling of further embarrassment at being invited to display their ignorance in open discussion. Subsequently they may be ready to join a house group, or a family-based learning group. In one parish there is an informal 'Bring and Share' evening on one Saturday a month, when people of all ages share a meal together and also share their news and concerns.

2.19 Opportunities for following up contacts with children and families need to be considered and, if they are appropriate to parish needs and resources, to be carefully planned and implemented. Many parishes train parents in the congregation to prepare other parents for the baptism of their babies. In some these meetings include an opportunity to talk about the experiences of pregnancy and childbirth, and the job of being parents, as well as the meaning of baptism. Some congregations give a present to the baby at the baptism service, and the offer of a baby-sitting service, or help with organising a baby sitting circle. One parish held a baptism anniversary tea party for the families of all those baptised in the last year. A visit at each baptism anniversary until the child starts school is customary in many parishes, but only some visitors remember to invite the family to a church social event, or to tell them about the parent and toddler group, the crèche, the pre-school playgroup, or a pram service.

A rota for fetching and carrying children to groups and clubs is normal practice in one parish. Another arranges an occasional informal group for parents of older children where they can explore together their particular concerns. One rural area arranges a holiday club twice a year for children from its churches. Others arrange parish weekends or holiday weeks to which families are welcomed and encouraged to come. Increasingly the children are given a meaningful part in the programmes arranged. Many such activities are already happening in parishes, reaching out to the families and children in their communities. Regular church members sometimes forget that those on the fringes of church life will only have the confidence to join in with them if specific invitations are offered, together with the assurance that they can go with, or meet up with, people whom they already know.

2.20 In one very small market town, an ageing Mothers' Union group was bemoaning the fact that none of the young mums came to join them. After discussion with the Diocesan Adviser, it emerged that their concern was about the lack of young people to carry on the traditions that had meant so much to them. They expressed surprise that most of the young mothers would never have been to Sunday school, let alone church, and therefore felt very awkward about coming to church even for their baby's baptism. So plans were made for a Teddy Bears' Picnic to be held in the Rectory garden one summer's afternoon. They decided to invite all the under-fives and their mothers from the town. The children played under supervision while the mothers chatted together, and appropriate refreshments were provided.

They distributed a leaflet outlining the church services, the provisions made for children and adults at the church, and information on how to ask for baptism and confirmation. They also made sure that the mothers met the Rector by asking him to give out the leaflets.

The afternoon was a great success. Over the following twelve months invitations followed to other events, such as a toddlers' harvest service, a Christingle service, Mothering Sunday. Baptisms (infant and adult) have increased, and several families have become regular worshippers.

Similar stories could undoubtedly be repeated many times. Invitations to fathers are less common, and it could be advisable to arrange some special events for them in the first instance. Many fathers would welcome opportunities to talk together about what it means to be a parent today, and are as anxious as mothers to do what's best for their children.

'I used to sit around crying and feeling tired but the girls (at the mother and toddler club) dragged me out of it. They talked about how they felt, and some of their problems, and I knew I wasn't the only one who felt like bashing the kids or running out on them'. (From Mother and Toddler Club, *Joyce Donoghue (Unwin Paperbacks).)*

THE CHURCH'S CONCERN FOR CHILDREN IN SOCIETY

2.21   Of course the concern for children and families is not only met by the Church. Many Christians, amongst others, are involved professionally or in voluntary capacities in agencies and informal groups which care for families and help them. It is helpful if the children of the Church are aware of such activities and if opportunities are made to share in them when it is appropriate. Both adults and children may judge the Church by its concern or lack of concern over the issues surrounding children, and others, in society.

2.22   Can we worship the Jesus who welcomed the children and exhorted us to become childlike - while condoning, if only by our silence, child poverty, child labour and child abuse? Are we prepared to press for greater safety and greater opportunities for children? For some adults responsible for children in parts of Africa, for example, the important question is not 'Shall we admit children to Communion?' but 'How shall we manage to keep our children alive until they reach adulthood?' Even in the United Kingdom there is cause for concern as the 1987 edition of *Social Trends* (HMSO) shows a wider gap between rich and poor. (Between 1976 and 1984 the income of the bottom two-fifths of households fell from 10 per cent. to 6 per cent. of the total, while the top fifth's income rose from 44 per cent. to 49 per cent. of the whole. We note that taxes and benefits reduced the gap.) In 1985 almost 109,000 homeless families were accepted by local authorities, as against 89,000 in 1983. In this country today 80,000 people are claiming supplementary benefit.

If we take seriously the commands of Jesus about children, we must share in prayerful and practical concern for all that prevents children in this world living their lives to the full. So we need as a Church at national and local level to be concerned with issues of food for the hungry, poverty, housing, safety, child labour, and the exploitation of children as it affects children and families in other countries and in our own. Jesus said nothing about only the children of the faithful being part of the kingdom. He appears to have welcomed them unreservedly: to have fed the multitude, not just the faithful few. In the past the Church expressed its concern about children, particularly by the establishment of Church schools and the care of orphans. Perhaps today we need to add to this by seeking effective ways of championing the cause of children and families in our own society and in the world?

2.23   At a time of change in our own society, with our family patterns changing, as we have seen in chapter 1, the Church also needs to give guidance and assurance about the importance and place of the stable family. The fact of failure and sin does not excuse us from presenting and teaching an acceptable model to our members. At the risk of being accused of saying 'Don't do as I do, do as I tell you' there is still a place for putting before society an ideal of a family in which children are brought up by both parents and where the children are presented with models of loyalty and self-giving love. Of course, there is need to care for those for whom this ideal is not a reality. But we must 'never let the actual take the heart out of the ideal'. Parents need support to maintain their marriages and bring up their children. Children need to see examples of happy, faithful, Christian marriages. Young people need to learn about the commitment of marriage and about ways of achieving happy family life. They need to learn relationship skills and Christian teaching of forgiveness and reconciliation. There is work here for both the school and for the voluntary groups of the Church. We tend to regret the passing of the old ways; we need to look for ways of supporting and enriching newer patterns.

2.24   The Church's mission is surely concerned with such issues, and the Church is more likely to be judged by people outside its own community on its attitude towards such situations than on the niceties of the ordering of Church worship. We are anxious to show that the Church is a place of caring and of faith. We need our children to have a model with which to grow up which will be satisfying and challenging to them as they take responsibility for the leadership of the Church. The Church which is striving to attain its ideals is one in which children will find a place and families will find security and enrichment.

RECOMMENDATIONS

1 Parishes, deaneries and dioceses undertaking children's evangelistic missions should examine the appropriate basis for them, with special reference to follow-up work, family involvements and peer group pressures.

2 The Church, nationally and locally, should actively support the efforts of uniformed groups to evaluate the moral and spiritual aspects of their work with children.

3 Parishes should consider how they can best support the best traditions of Christian marriage and family life, while affirming their active and sensitive concern and care for all for whom this is not a reality.

4 Boards of General Synod should include the consideration of children's needs and experience in their Reports to Synod whenever this is appropriate.

5 The Board of Mission and Unity and the Board of Education should explore as a matter of urgency appropriate ways to enable children and leaders to respond to a multi-ethnic society.

3. What Sort of Model?

A COMPLEX PICTURE

'What I like about Church is when it is finished and it's time to chat to everyone'. (Five-year-old)
'I looked round the church today - why does everyone look so sad? Why can't we have time to get to know each other?' (Eight-year-old)

3.1 We need as a Church to look at our methods of reaching families and children outside the Church or on the edge of it. We also need to look at the style of learning and worship and activity which we offer to those within it, and to those whom we hope to encourage to join with us. So in this chapter we are concentrating on the domestic aspects of children's work - the style and pattern of Christian nurture that we offer to those children who are associated with our parishes; who come either with or through one or more parents, or by themselves, but in some sense identify with a particular congregation.

3.2 It is sometimes argued by those who look at this area nationally that abolishing all traditional forms of 'Sunday school' is the only genuine hope for the future. While we continue to try to work a nineteenth-century model, they argue, we shall not even begin to touch the real needs of Christian nurture in what some people see to be the secularised, post-Christian society of the 1990s.

3.3 Another school of thought suggests that the only real place for Christian nurture is in the home, and that the vast majority of what resources are available should be channelled into supporting Christian parents in this task.

3.4 A third school argues that real nurture only takes place when children are accepted as part of the one worshipping congregation and few, if any, special concessions are made to them.

3.5   We would reply that to push any one of these radical conclusions as 'the' solution ignores the complexity of needs faced by our parishes. Coming to our thinking from a practical basis of day-to-day work with children's leaders, clergy and parishes, we are acutely aware that the situations in which work with children, and adults, has to take place vary enormously.

3.6   First, there are differences in the kinds of environment in which parishes are set. For example, the church in a scattered rural area, sharing a priest with three or four other parishes, with few children and many elderly retired people in the parish, is in a very different situation from the suburban parish which has a vicar and curate, a large number of worshipping families and many eager, efficient leaders for its many activities. Attitudes towards 'in-comers' or 'the old stagers' or 'the noisy children' will also need to be taken into account. So too will the buildings which are available to those involved in Christian nurture activities. Some parishes are provided with hall and meeting rooms, black-out facilities and electrical points, washrooms and space for craft-work. Others within the same diocese may have only the use of the church itself, with the consequent problems of trying to adapt it for children's activities and to find suitable times for them to meet. In many rural areas church buildings are removed from the main centres of population, and arranging transport can be acutely difficult, especially where each village may have but one service on a Sunday, ranging across the month from 8 a.m. to 10 a.m. to 6.30 p.m.
  There is no way in which we can talk about single solutions as if there were uniform schemes which could be applied to all parishes. They would fail to acknowledge the complexity and variety of factors any parish has to consider in assessing its contribution to Christian nurture.

3.7   In addition, it is our conviction that in every parish an individual or a small group of people will be the primary channel through which the whole congregation's concern for the valuing of its children will need to be poured. Any group, any individual is rightly the concern of the whole community, but that concern must be expressed through the particular interest and work of other individuals. Were 'Sunday schools' or their like not to exist, most churches looking to the spiritual growth and development of their members would still recognise children as one of the many particular groups requiring distinctive help and support.

3.8　To reject apparently simple radical solutions and to recognise the difficulties faced by parishes is not the same as saying that everything is generally satisfactory, or that if we continued to do what we do now, but did it better, that would be a sufficient solution. If our leaders were better trained, our resources more professional and sophisticated, our facilities modernised and improved, then would the future be largely assured? Again, without denying the value of any of these, we believe the situation that confronts us is a great deal more complex and demanding.

3.9　With all these necessary preliminaries, we believe that it is an appropriate time to look very carefully at the models we use in our work with children and to seek for ways in which these might be extended, adapted, enriched for our present circumstances. Most Christians are familiar with models like that of the Body of Christ for the whole Church. They may be less familiar with models for the Church's task in Christian education.

THE 'SCHOOL' MODEL

> *'School was made for learning, not praising God, except in assembly where you are learning (stories) and praising God.'*

3.10　It is not surprising that the Church's work with children should largely fix on the school model, remembering that the original Sunday schools were schools on Sunday which offered working children the basic skill of reading, alongside some Christian instruction. But as a contemporary model for the Church, the secular school has its limitations. Despite changes in educational methods, the understanding of school which many adults hold is of an outmoded and formal style long since superseded. In the same way, many adults can only think of the Church's work with children in terms of the style of Sunday school teaching which they themselves received. For children there are implications that Christian learning is something which you finish and leave behind you in the same way as you leave school. It appears to them that adult status means that you do not engage in learning in the Church. Associations surrounding 'the Sunday school' are therefore not helpful.

3.11   We need to be aware of the fundamental differences between day school and the Church's children's groups. Schooling in England is compulsory, highly organised and structured, and professionally staffed; children generally accept that they have to attend. Congregations and potential leaders have to recognise that this does not apply to the Church's work with children. Groups are voluntary, loosely structured, and staffed by volunteers who are largely without formal teaching qualifications. Many children come irregularly. They don't accept that they have to attend and their parents are often not interested in ensuring long-term commitment either for their children or (perhaps even more significantly) for themselves.

3.12   The school model also tends to put the teacher or leader into the role of the one who knows and the children into the position of those who need to know; teacher and taught, instructor and instructed. For many reasons this is not always helpful. Many voluntary teachers know their inadequacy to fulfil this position and, because of it, are put off from volunteering help and support. Many young teachers and helpers, who themselves do not realise their inadequacies, are expected to pass on knowledge which they either don't possess or don't properly understand. And so a more and more simplified version of the faith is passed on.

In day schools, which provide the model, many teachers increasingly spend time working not just as instructors but also with groups of children, drawing out their ideas and knowledge, helping them to extend and explore their experiences. The skills required for this approach to education are more demanding than those required for formal instruction.

3.13   Nevertheless, while voluntary teachers need knowledge and understanding, many potential leaders and most teenage helpers would feel much greater confidence if they could see that their primary role is to be alongside the children, sharing in their excitement and learning as fellow-learners, fellow-worshippers, fellow-members of the Church community. They see already that they do not have all to give and the children all to receive. Although the time spent just in the children's groups is usually very short, relationships are based on smaller numbers, closer knowledge and more personal involvement than is possible in a large day school. At best children's leaders recognise that they are sharing in a venture with the children - the journey of faith. We rightly take much from the school model, but we should not let it dominate or restrict our thinking about what is possible.

THE 'FAMILY' MODEL

'God is very big, but not as big as my Daddy' (Three-year-old).

'I don't like going to Church because the vicar doesn't speak so we understand it. But it doesn't mean I don't believe in God because my mum brought me up to believe in God and I got Christian and I wanted to' (Eight-year-old).

3.14   It is difficult to know whether the 'Family' model really exists in the way that most Anglicans would recognise the Sunday school pattern. But whether we talk of family nurture, family services or family metaphors and images, this has been a striking and in many ways enriching addition to the Anglican vocabulary.

3.15   We therefore need to explore the significance of the family as a model for Christian nurture. Dr Gloria Durka of Fordham University has defined the family as

'any small group of people who consider themselves bound to each other by enduring ties, and who are responsible for each other's wellbeing.'

Although we may be used to thinking of families as being

'any association or relationship in which a child is cared for and brought up by an adult' *(The Child in the Church: Understanding Christian Nurture)*

we must remind ourselves of the rich variety of families in our society and in our churches.

3.16   In a family we have potentially a group of people who are naturally dependent on one another, and whose various skills and knowledge are used for the good of the whole group. At any time the leadership may move from one person to another as ideas occur and decisions are made by different members. Power may be exercised by the 'weakest' as well as by the 'strongest' members, though not always deliberately or consciously: for example, the needs of the small baby or elderly grandparent may be the determining factor in many decisions. In most families some activities are undertaken by the *whole* family, and indeed the things which are regularly done together help to bind the family, provided that the signs are recognised when an activity is being outgrown by some of the members. Some activities are rightly pursued by individual members alone or with friends outside the family; these can be enriching for the quality of relationships within the family, as can the introduction of friends and new relatives into the group. With these changes, however, may also come problems of adaptation.

This is a picture of the 'ideal' family, of course. But it can be a situation of conflict and violence, of individuals with scarcely any interest or concern for one another, where little or nothing is done as a corporate activity. In the 'best' of families there are arguments and pain as well as harmony and joy; the home can be the place where the worst sides of our natures are all too apparent, and the frustrations of our lives in the wider world are taken out on one another.

3.17   Small children learn by imitating the skills and attitudes of the rest of the family, watching and listening to them, as well as by some direct instruction and by hearing family stories. Encouragement and delight in one another's achievements, acceptance of each member in his or her own right, a sense of security in knowing where each member belongs and what is expected of him or her: all these will give a safe base for venturing and exploring beyond the limits of the family group. Conflicting attitudes, or a wide variation in what is expected of a child, will damage the child's sense of security and confidence. Families usually have rules or standards of behaviour (some unspoken) which members are expected to keep. Methods have to be worked out to deal with failures to keep them, and with disagreements, arguments and demands for changes. Ways of helping families are explored in chapter 5; our concern here is to explore the family as a model for our life and learning in the Church.

3.18   In the image of the Church as a family, there are some attractive ideals for considering Christian nurture. For example, a Church can arrange some activities for all its members to share, some just for particular groups within the fellowship. The model suggests a need to work out appropriate ways of sharing skills and leadership, to recognise the possible power of the weakest members, and to sort out ways of passing on stories and appropriate rituals. It indicates a fellowship of mutually dependent people, affirming the importance of the individual members, and sharing in the joys and sorrows of the important events in their lives. The Church family, like the human family, has to cope with argument, dissension and change, and yet remain secure in its basic bonds. It needs to be outward-looking, ready to welcome new members, willing to involve itself in interests which lie outside its concern for its own well-being.

3.19 The children of the Church family need to be recognised as members of its fellowship, sharing in activities when appropriate, provided with separate groups when helpful to them, and encouraged to learn from the stories, behaviour and attitudes of their elders in formal and informal ways. The growth of family services (liturgical and non-liturgical), family fun days, and parish family holidays shows the developing awareness of the richness of this 'model'.

3.20 There are, however, limitations in using this model – as in using any model. Many people today feel families tend to be exclusive and self-absorbed, despite their efforts to be outward-looking. Some people's experience of family life has been so crippling that they find the image is disabling in itself. Above all, despite many attempts to describe the Church family as being the *whole* family of the Church in a particular place, many single people still feel that its emphasis and its activities are concerned only with family groups – parents and children – and that their needs are neither acknowledged nor met. This is reflected in an article and consequent letters in the *Methodist Recorder*. One correspondent says:

> 'The trouble with using "family" as an image for the Church (apart from the fact that every time I hear it I feel like a pacifist hearing the Church referred to as "God's army") is that it implies that family life is superior to all other ways of life, an idea which has no support in the Gospel.' (*Methodist Recorder*, April 9, 1987.)

Other single correspondents, however, have no problem about seeing themselves as being members of the family of the Church. We could deduce from this that the quality of the Church family will affect people's perception of their place in it, but we have to note the frequency of occasions when single members of happy welcoming congregations have been bewildered by invitations to join in Church Family events: 'I didn't know it was for me,' they say. Nor should we underestimate the potential pain and sense of exclusion for those who are widowed and those whose marriages have broken; nor the difficulties and conflict of loyalties for those whose partners are indifferent or hostile to the Church.

3.21 What may be helpful in these circumstances is another model to extend the variety of our practice, to give a stimulus to our imagination and to provide another pattern against which our present practice can be evaluated. We need to feel free enough and confident enough to explore other models, to see what may be safely relinquished in our present approach and what may be adapted and enriched for the future. This is not to undermine or under-value what people are already doing. We find many voluntary leaders ready to think afresh, partly because they feel - often instinctively - that they would like to do more than the present pattern seems to allow.

THE 'PILGRIM CHURCH' MODEL

3.22 The image of the Church as a pilgrim community adds new dimensions which may be helpful. While the school model can all too easily be interpreted as teacher and taught and the family model may feel too restricted, the pilgrim community comprises a band of people all sharing in and learning from common experience.

3.23 Imagine a group of people of all ages going for a long walk together. At times the children and adults will walk along together, talking as they go, sharing stories with first one person and then another, each observing different things and sharing their discoveries. At times the children will lag behind and some of the adults will have to wait for them or urge them on. Sometimes the smallest children may ask to be carried. At other times, though, the children will dash ahead making new discoveries and may, perhaps, pull the adults along to see what they have found. Some adults may well behave like these children, of course. For all there will be times of progress and times of rest and refreshment, time to admire the view, and times of plodding on, and the eventual satisfaction of arrival at their destination.

3.24 Of course, a pilgrimage is something more than a hike. Traditionally it is a group of people of all kinds and ages united in reaching a common goal. They stop at significant places on the way. They exchange their own stories, and share past experiences and memories of those who have gone before them. They look forward to the rest of the journey and to reaching their ultimate destination.

3.25 When we apply this image to the community of the Church we see that there are still those who teach and those who learn - but the teaching comes from all members of the community and the learning just as much from informal as formal situations. While this is sometimes rather grandly labelled 'inter-generational learning', the principle is simple. A congregation in which all the members are engaged on some joint venture, whether it be activity based on fund-raising or shared learning, inevitably finds young learning from old and old learning from young. As in a pilgrim group, the young may find some situations easier to surmount than their elders. Sometimes they lead the way and are not always the followers-on. Who learns new hymns more quickly?

The pilgrim model suggests learning from shared experience and shared stories. It implies developing new skills, adapting and changing attitudes, and looking for new visions. We are all slow to recognise as adult Christians that this sort of learning is a life-long process. The success of adult Christian Education courses is a step in the right direction; the pilgrim community suggests this is not an optional extra but a real necessity for all.

3.26   We are learning, as we have seen, a great deal from the family model of Christian nurture. But families can become inward-looking, can concentrate solely on their own internal lives, can be too restrictive for the growing life of children and adults. These are dangers we need to guard against, just as we must recognise the numbers of children who do not find the family image a source of security and comfort, and who may also need a wider community to which to relate. At best the pilgrim Church provides just such a wider grouping; people of different styles and ages, people of widely ranging sympathies and ideals, people whose experience and concerns are of use to the children travelling with them, and with whom the children can share their insights and skills. Yet how often do we create the situations where the two may meet and share?

3.27   What comes through time and again in the pilgrim model is that all those involved on the journey are inextricably bound up one with the other. All are in some sense responsible one for the other, all are learning and sharing in the communal life. The whole body is impoverished by the loss of any of its members. All learn from each other. All need more than one kind of knowledge, experience or skill. Nurture which does not include experience and worship as well as learning will always fail to create real growth. At the same time we need to be sensitive and supportive to those adults who are apprehensive about this kind of involvement.

3.28   Any programme of Christian nurture focused solely on knowledge - biblical, doctrinal or moral - is inadequate without an equal concentration on worship, prayer and growth in the spiritual life. So it is as important to say 'Our children are not taught to pray' as the much more frequently heard 'Our children aren't getting taught Bible stories today'. It would also be good to hear the complaint 'Our children don't get real experience of what being a Christian is all about'. Some difficult questions follow. Is our Church an environment where children can absorb the importance of all these elements of the Christian life? What opportunities do we provide for children to work alongside adults in a joint venture? What quality of experience of worship, Christian learning and the Christian life does your church provide for its children? And the question is not just about what your Sunday school or family service provides, but about what is provided by your church in all its variety and life.

3.29 The same sort of questions apply to the content of our course materials. Some critics believe that children are not getting a real diet of Christian teaching on which to feed and grow. Sadly what they often mean by this is a heavy dose of random Bible stories, the geography of first-century Palestine and Church history. We would agree that children often do not get a sense of the cutting edge of Christianity, the strength of its ideals and the reality of its demands. We need to establish from the beginning the essence of the great salvation story as it is lived out in the Bible, and as it shapes our understanding of our journey.

We would also argue that children are not given sufficient opportunity to become instruments of their own learning, to share in discussion, to match their stories to the stories of God's people, to contribute to joint activity, to make real contributions to worship. Throughout we are arguing for a better diet of learning, experience and worship in the lives of our children, in a community where all are valued for themselves, where it is leader and fellow-learners rather than teacher and taught, where all are involved in the enterprise, all partners on the journey, all seeking to grow through greater understanding, deeper worship and a wider experience of Christian living. Some parishes have already begun to use new ways of learning together, as we shall see in the next chapter. Others feel ready to try out new styles, or to change the emphasis in what they already do. Others need to begin to look for suitable opportunities to bring children and adults together, if only on an occasional basis.

3.30 At the same time there will be landmarks and refreshment on the way, through the grace given to the children and adults in their sacramental life. The significance of the baptismal experience needs to be marked by the congregation as a whole wherever possible. The importance of the Eucharist in binding, strengthening and incorporating the members of the Church and in re-living the salvation experience is self-evident. The question of the appropriateness of Communion for the children of the Church remains unresolved (see page 51), but any view of Christian nurture which suggests the inclusion of children as fellow pilgrims and the interdependence of children and adults is bound to raise the question anew.

IMPLICATIONS

3.31   The implications of all this have been spelled out before. Three areas keep recurring. First, this understanding of Christian nurture requires adults to recognise that they are fellow-learners with children. It requires them to acknowledge their shared responsibility for each other's nurture by sharing their experience, and sharing in worship and learning. It is sad how rarely older people recognise that their presence and attitude in worship are the most influential models for children. And when children ask themselves 'What does it really mean to be a Christian?' their answer is nearly always 'Like Mrs X or Mr Y.'

3.32   Second, it means giving much greater thought to the reasoning behind our parish worship and ministry. The younger members of the pilgrimage will always be wanting to know 'where are we going?' 'what are we doing?' 'why are we doing it?' 'what is it for?' 'why are we going with these people?' Indeed, their challenges and unease may well express the unspoken and unacknowledged questions of many adults. If we can't answer these questions with some conviction, then it is not surprising that children set off in other directions. This is a long-term but urgent task.

3.33   Third, the pilgrim Church requires the right sort of knowledge. It is knowledge needed for the journey, therefore knowledge related to the immediate tasks, and knowledge linking the stories and traditions of the elders in the community to the road ahead. If their companions offer the children knowledge which is inappropriate or irrelevant to them, the children will quickly lose interest and look elsewhere for satisfaction.

RECOMMENDATIONS

1 PCCs, wherever possible, should plan at least one venture for the coming year in which adults and children are involved together in learning and exploring what it means to be followers 'in the Way', and should develop a continuing pattern for learning together.

2 Diocesan Education Officers (for adult, youth and children's work) should actively explore and implement ways of creating joint learning experiences for children and adults.

4. Growing in Faith

DEVELOPING FAITH

4.1 *'When I was a child.... I thought of God as a man, an ancient grandfather, like my vicar but more so, kind as a lamb, with a wonderful home containing many mansions and a spacious garden complete with glassy sea, but who always had time to look at me and in whose 'house' I felt special by virtue of its aura as a holy place and my importance in it as head chorister.*

I enjoyed going to church - lots of people to talk to me - both young and old - I was often involved, important, even leading Sunday school, in the choir, in the confirmation class and in the readings, the processions and the singing in church.'

4.2 This recollection of childhood by one young man highlights not only the concerns of 'children's work' or 'Sunday school', but also the way in which we all, children and adults, discover and grow in faith. One of the experiences all Christians identify is that their faith grows and changes. Nor is this true of Christian faith alone. There are times when faith feels strong and times when its weakness is the most obvious quality; sometimes faith seems easy and at other times it can be difficult. The events and experiences of life have a vital influence on these different stages of faith, as do the people with whom we come into contact. We need to remind ourselves that the same sorts of things are happening to children. The process of growth in faith is common to children and adults.

4.3 There is yet another dimension to this growth. It is not only the strength of our faith which changes; the style, the way we hold it, also develops. Many of us observe in general terms how children's views of faith move from being affected primarily by the adults with whom they are in closest contact to being influenced in attitudes and values much more by their own age group and the close community in which they belong. Later there is often a move to a more searching stage as they try to create a more individual understanding based on new and wider experience, using an increased ability to think rationlly and critically. Out of this searching may emerge a more mature and satisfying faith which can cope with tensions and paradox and which continues to grow through searching and questioning. This is increasingly being recognised as a life-long process. Neither the strength nor the style of our faith ever stops developing and each individual needs much support and understanding to encourage that development.

4.4   For a long time our understanding of individuals growing in the Church has been largely in terms of intellectual development rather than faith development. Though we have become aware of important factors in the process, we have not really had the means to see exactly how faith develops through these stages and how best to encourage its positive growth. Many churches fear that they lose contact with children between the ages of nine and twelve when they most need help to move on to develop a more complex but richer understanding and faith for themselves. At this age also they begin to encounter the apparent certainty of 'scientific truth', the complexities and uncertainties of which only become apparent much later.

Two Christian educators, John Westerhoff and James Fowler, have provided some insight into this faith development which could enrich and liberate much of our thinking. We are not uncritical of the claims made for this work and we are conscious that it has largely developed in a society very different from our own. But their analysis of faith development is an attempt to look thoughtfully and critically at how individuals might grow in faith, and we cannot afford to ignore it in our concern to understand and improve Christian nurture in the Church of England. In this context it is impossible to do more than sketch in the outlines of their thinking and point to some further reading.

4.5   Westerhoff describes sequential development through four 'styles of faith'. He likens growth in faith to the way a tree grows.

> 'A tree in its first year is a complete and whole tree, and a tree with three rings is not a better tree but only an expanded tree. In a similar way, one

style of faith is not a better or greater faith than another.'

(Will Our Children Have Faith?)

The tree, if it has a suitable environment, does its own growing and develops its own characteristics; it acquires new rings in a slow, gradual manner over the whole of its life – but rings are added, none are eliminated. People expand from one style of faith to another when the proper environment, experiences and interactions are present. This happens gradually and slowly, adding each new style to the previous ones.

4.6 John Westerhoff describes four styles of faith. We begin as young children with an 'experienced faith', feeling inevitably part of what is around us, dependent on experience and interaction.

'The child explores and tests, imagines and creates, observes and copies, experiences and reacts.'

So faith first comes not through theological words but through the experiences like those of trust, love and acceptance related to those words. The question is not 'What do I tell my child?' but 'What is it like to be Christian with my child?' says Westerhoff.

Then comes 'affiliative faith'.

We need to belong to, and participate in, an identity-conscious community of faith'

with opportunities to deepen religious feelings through creative activities, to share in the community's stories, and to experience awe, wonder and mystery. Beliefs and attitudes are more consciously taken over from a significant other person or valued group; there is a need at this time for acceptance and belonging.

The third style is a 'searching faith' which strives to work out a consistent personal faith with reference to an authority within rather than that of other people. Typically, there will need to be elements of doubt and critical judgement; a need for experimentation, as alternative understandings and traditions are explored; a need to commit their lives to people and to causes.

Finally there is an 'owned faith' which holds the tension of truth viewed from different perspectives and finds new meaning in myth, symbol and ritual.

'Now people most want to put their faith into personal and social action, and they are willing and able to stand up for what they believe, even against the community of their nurture.'

This movement from experienced faith through to owned faith is what Westerhoff sees as conversion, a major change in a person's total behaviour which may be sudden or gradual. He says that

> 'to reach owned faith (our full potential) is a long pilgrimage in which we need to be provided with an environment and experiences that encourage us to act in ways that assist our expansion of faith'

but that wherever we are on that pilgrimage, none is outside Christ's redeeming grace.

4.7   Some simple observations immediately spring from this analysis. Many churches are deeply concerned that they are losing contact with children at an ever-younger age. The tension between these styles of faith, experienced, affiliative and searching, may occur at ever-younger ages, when the components of resolution and growth are often not available to the child or comprehensible to him or her. Styles of faith, however, are not about fitting a style to a particular age group. Typically, in Westerhoff's judgement, many adults are in an affiliative style of faith. We therefore need to provide a variety of Christian learning experiences in our churches.

4.8   James Fowler conducted in-depth interviews with people of all ages to elicit the data for his research into faith development (which in itself has caused us to reflect on the importance of putting aside time to examine where we are in our faith and to recognise and appreciate the faith of others). He has come to understand faith as a verb, something we do. He posits seven developmental stages through which our 'faithing' may pass, the first three or four of which generally belong to childhood. A brief outline of these can be found on page 52.

4.9   The basic idea that the faith of the individual develops in style as well as in content and intensity seems consistent with our experience, and is confirmed by the experience and research of the Christian educators we have quoted, and of others. Certain implications for our Church life follow from this understanding. There is a need not only to think in terms of supporting and deepening different styles of faith but also to provide opportunities which may help people move from one style to another. We cannot *force* people to new styles or stages of faith. Our task is to provide the most appropriate experiences, and to be ready with sensitive support at transition times.

Looking at Westerhoff's styles, the earliest, 'experienced', style of faith makes demands on parents, other adults and members of congregations whom children will copy, and with whom they will interact. An 'affiliative faith' requires considerable contact with other members of the faith community and activities to reinforce a feeling of belonging, to share its stories and provide occasions for experiencing awe and wonder. The 'searching faith' may be encouraged by opportunities to work alongside adults, to go out and meet other communities and individuals of faith, to challenge and question and talk through new ideas. At a particular stage Church members must be enabled or prompted to question themselves, to address themselves to the questions of those outside the Church, and to support others in their radical action in the world.

> *'I think of God as a friend, as a guardian who loves me... It's a pity adults find it so hard to believe. They are afraid and they don't want to face God but that's completely wrong because God says He will always forgive us. I think Jesus finds it very sad when adults lose the faith that children have.'*
> (Eleven-year-old boy in Helen House, Oxford)

> *'I picture God as the religion books say, an all-knowing and loving God... an all-loving and all-powerful person - and a person! ...I consider God like a lifeline, a friend, because during the day you're working around and I talk to him. I think, and in thinking, I talk to him. I believe there is a God and he hears what I'm saying and knows what I'm thinking and is there to help me...'*
> (Woman in early thirties. From *Life Maps*, Fowler and Keen)

4.10   One does not have to accept these particular academic analyses of Westerhoff and Fowler to recognise that children and adults grow in faith, and it is not suggested that these stages are directly identifiable with any chronological age. On the contrary: a fifty-year-old and a five-year-old might easily have the same stage of style of faith, although their knowledge and experience differ. Nor is it the case that one stage has more value than another; rather like the changes of state that overtake H_2O with the benefit of heat-from ice to water to steam - they are different. It is clearly of fundamental importance for the growth of faith that we accept the *way* children have faith. It cannot be the same as for adults, and to inflict an adult's 'interpretation', 'truth' or 'story' in preference to the child's own leads at best to confusion. In Christian faith, a conversion experience - a sudden development - may also have its place. As a Church we place value on all faith. 'Do you believe and trust...?' we ask at baptism, and then we acknowledge membership of the Lord's family:

'We are members together of the body of Christ; we are children of the same heavenly Father.'

Faith development research emphasises again and again the importance of taking seriously the stage of faith of each individual.

4.11   Growing in faith is a process common to children and adults. It takes place continuously within the Church and without it, during the 'children's work' and in worship. If the children, especially, are to grow, a congregation must be asking of all its activities, not just the 'children's work': 'Is it helping the children's faith to grow, or impending it? What else should we do for the children (and for the adults) to help them grow in faith?' The natural development process of faith development is best encouraged within a faith community where development, learning and change are the norm and where equal attention is given by the whole community to learning, Christian experience and worship.

4.12   Our increasing understanding of 'growth' in the life of faith rephrases many of our questions about our work and relationships with children in our church, about how we pass on ideas and about the practical arrangements we make for children in the life of our church. How do we talk about God as the understanding of children and young people changes? We perceive ever more clearly the importance for children of individuals within the faith community who act as friend and example. We need to see how adults can be available to children, offering seeds developed in their own lives of faith which can grow with a child, rather than presenting a childish formula which will have to be slowly - or suddenly - unlearned later. Thus the images we give cannot be closed, so God may not be presented as just human, nor just male, nor just anything, nor as completely comprehended by anyone. And if we are to provide the right environment for expanding through 'stages' or 'styles' of faith, we must be able to let our stories and our liturgy communicate. To tell an enjoyable story from the Bible is not to guarantee growth in faith. If, however, we are passing on a story that is real to us, if our stories speak to children's experience, if they are part of the Church they see and if their use is consistent with their biblical and theological context, then we may have the opportunity to take on the germination of seeds sown in the enjoyment and imagination rendered by the story.

43

ALL-AGE LEARNING

'To me all adults were "they" and although one didn't take all "they" said as Gospel, it was often wise to pretend that one did, otherwise parents, or God, that rather tiresome old man up in the sky, might see fit to punish one. Unfortunately, there were very few sympathetic listeners among "them", discussions about religion weren't done in our circle.' (Adult reflecting on childhood, from *The Original Vision*, Edward Robinson (RERU).)

4.13   What we are arguing here is that the nurture of children is parallel to and also continuous with the education and growth of teenagers and adults. As adults and children work together questions may well be raised which adults need to develop and pursue at a different level in an adult group. It appears – both in theory and practice – that much of our learning and growing could be done in all-age groups. Efforts spent developing methods and materials for all-age learning in a variety of situations would be well invested. In many of our churches the congregations are small and the numbers of children accordingly tiny. Some small congregations which have found it difficult to organise their children's work into a traditional 'Sunday school', have changed to meetings for adults and children together. The group has become more viable, and the richness of ideas and sharing have enabled them to grow as a community and travel together along the way of faith. Larger congregations have also discovered the advantages of regular or occasional learning events.

4.14   In one United Reformed Church the following pattern is used:

'Each Sunday, two forms of worship are offered to the congregation. A conventional preaching service is held for those who prefer this, but an alternative is offered to those who wish to participate in exploring a theme through a variety of activities. This alternative is called 'Worship in the Round'. Everybody joins in a twenty- to thirty-minute family service to conclude the session.

Worship in the Round is attended by 20 to 40 adults and eight to 12 children. The shape and content of the session is determined by a group of four to five worshippers who meet several times during the previous month. *Partners in Learning* themes are taken as a starting point and the preaching service covers roughly the same ground.

Sometimes the children and adults are together, sometimes apart. More often, the session starts with some introductory activity in which both children and adults can share, after which they separate for more detailed study and experience at appropriate levels.'

44

4.15   In one group of several parishes in a country area, children and adults collect together one Saturday a month and go to one of the churches in turn to explore the theme for the Sunday service. They prepare for the worship, making banners, devising drama, practising hymns and songs as the theme best lends itself, and incorporating their work into the Sunday service in that church.

4.16   A parish contemplating all-age work for the first time might like to try a one-off event first. A three-hour workshop and worship for adults and children could be held on Good Friday. Preparation for the celebration of Christmas or the patronal festival, or to explore the themes for Christian Aid or One World Week, would all provide opportunities for an all-age activity day. One parish held its first all-age day on a Saturday in the hall and church of another parish in the diocese, and explored the theme of 'Belonging', making collages in small groups of all ages, working at a Bible study together in the same groups, then separating into adult groups to discuss further and children's groups to prepare drama. At the concluding act of worship the children presented their drama, and the adults offered the main ideas of their discussion through subjects for intercession.

4.17   One suburban church organised a programme of all-age learning for Lent, taking the theme of 'The Easter People'. Each Sunday a parish breakfast was arranged for those who wished to stay after the eight o'clock service, and for those who came before the learning programme. Groups then met in a nearby school to explore the theme in music, drama, art work and Bible study. All the groups were open to people of all ages. Parish Communion followed this learning activity. On Easter Day the work of all the groups was offered in the Parish Communion service.

4.18   We do not believe that this approach is a universal panacea, but we are encouraged by the growth of genuinely all-age parish programmes in which young and old - families, retired couples, single people - share together in learning about their faith, with the focus often but not entirely on the younger element. The Church, and the average church congregation, contains more than any other group the possibilities for *all* generations to meet and learn together. Many families today are without, or far from, grandparents, aunts and uncles; many children have no siblings or only ones of the same sex; as chapter 1 has reminded us, there are many single-parent families, single people, widowed and divorced: all meet in the Church on common ground. It is a truism that a clear, unpretentious message and more creative approach to learning intended for young people often strikes a chord with older members as well. Have we begun to consider the implications of this fact for our general life and development?

This does not mean that opportunities for more 'intellectual' learning should never be provided for those who need it, nor that children should be denied all opportunities for learning with their peers. But we particularly look in the near future for a widespread sharing of the practical ideas involved in all-age learning, based on a realistic understanding of the way faith develops and grows.

4.19 Even where all-age activities as such are not possible, ways need to be found of integrating children into church life. Here is a description of the way one parish tackled this:

'The Sunday school tackles a number of projects during the year, each complete in itself, and all related to one another. Built into each project will be some definite point of contact with the older members of the church. Sometimes it will be simply that the congregation is invited to view the "end product" over coffee after the service. More strikingly, perhaps, the children are seen and heard in the Eucharist itself. In a recent project on the Holy Communion, for instance, children led the Intercessions – the older ones speaking what they had themselves written, the younger ones illustrating each section with the help of a revolving pentagon they had made. As the climax of a project on "Bread", each child kneaded a roll at the beginning of the Parish Communion. These were then cooked and carried, still steaming, in the Offertory procession to the altar to be used for the Communion. A project on "Living Stones" involved the children in inviting everyone to sign a cardboard "brick" as they returned from the altar – the bricks later to be built into a church where all could spot their brick and recognise their part in the whole.

'This brings us to the other side of the coin. Opening up the area of children's work to the older members of the congregation does not call simply for an interested, but essentially passive, response. Of course, it will help enormously if adults can learn to accept the children's part in worship as a valid and valuable contribution. If this leads to deeper reflection on their part, so much the better. But they should be more actively involved.

'At the simplest level it is often possible, with a little imagination, to devise from time to time projects which will involve members of the congregation joining Sunday school for one or two sessions; perhaps the sacristan, or a flower-arranger, or a tenor from the choir. The learning will not all be on one side! Or, again, a new look at the staffing of the Sunday school may help. How many people are discouraged from offering their services by their inability to make a weekly commitment throughout the year? We have found that the "project" approach has developed a far greater team sense. Because the system allows people to opt for greater or lesser involvement according to their other, changing, commitments, we have been able to benefit from the help of several who could not have joined a more rigid system.'

4.20   Another parish involves 70 people in leadership roles with the children, some members of each team being responsible for pastoral care, some for worship, some for the under-fives, and some for the projects undertaken.

4.21   More adults must find, or be helped to find, opportunities to link with the children's work in order that incidental opportunities may arise on the journey of faith for the remark, half-conversation or dialogue that carries the travellers on. The frequently heard, and painful, criticism of the Church as 'old-fashioned' or 'out-of-touch' suggests among other things, a lack of the 'Christian experience' element in the nurture we offer. Do our children get real experience of what being a Christian is all about? Christianity is a way of life, it is about the everyday, but everyday experiences and the issues and problems of life seldom figure in our worship or in our children's groups. It is noticeable when our Church families meet together how few adult Christians engage with the younger members to share experiences, views, ideas or stories. It may also be noted how few of our 'groups' – house groups, study groups or prayer groups – have the courage to include the children, and how few of the published Lent courses, for example, acknowledge the possible presence of children.

FAITH IN THE HOME

'I believe in God really because my mum and dad do' (Ten-year-old)

4.22   As we have seen, the greatest influence on a child's growth in faith is the home. Its importance is reinforced by the description of the earliest style of faith noted in 4.6 above. Most of the child's development and learning takes place here and the parents are therefore major partners in the process of nurture. The three elements of learning, experience and worship can be present in the home family; parents often seize on help, encouragement and support on those occasions when it is offered either through informal groups, or publications or suggestions from the Church and its leaders. Our Survey shows that the midweek church service for under-fives and parents is growing in popularity. Part of their value lies in the opportunity for parents to 'catch' ways of 'being Christian' with their young children. A recent consultation about such services, organised by one diocesan Children's Adviser, was attended by a surprisingly large number of people involved in such sessions and resulted in the sharing of an enormous variety of successful ideas.

4.23   The difficulties parents face in the home are very real. We do, however, find it difficult to help the 'typical' Church family, in ways which they find acceptable and can undertake without embarrassment in their own homes. (The newly converted family appears more at ease with explicitly religious activity together, perhaps because everything is new and different anyway, and also because their enthusiasm for a new way of life overcomes their inhibitions.) Some suggestions relating to parents are explored in chapter 5. It may be that we as adults need to find a spirituality which will match and bond together with our experience in daily living.

It is immediately apparent to those of us who work regularly with 'Church' families, let alone those on the fringe, that the traditional language of Christian explanation and teaching is totally alien to their ways of thinking. Christian clichés once had meaning because they tapped a residual level of experience and teaching; we can no longer assume any such background, and need to discipline ourselves to begin again the painful process of translating words such as 'repentance', 'grace', 'redemption', 'spirit', into metaphors and symbols that coincide with present-day areas of meaning.

SPIRITUALITY

'My way of praying is just praying with an open heart to Him so that I get the open answer back.' (Eleven-year-old in Helen House, Oxford).

4.24   The concentration on 'spirituality' in modern Religious Education may suggest it has a part to play in the Christian nurture of our children and adults. We welcome this recognition that the spiritual, the mysterious, the dynamic which provides a source of meaning and explanation, which enables people to be in touch with their own deepest feelings, which uses art, poetry and imagination to point beyond and within the material, has become a recognised element in thinking about Religious Education, and we have been grateful for the work of David Hay and the Religious Experience Research Project. It would be ironic if, just when schools were exploring the importance of spirituality and the experiental, participative aspects of learning, we should miss out on the very creative shared possibilities for the life of the Church. But we recognise that there is a danger in spirituality becoming an end in itself. Nor is it divorced from belief and doctrine. In a lecture to diocesan Children's Advisers in 1985, the Bishop of Jarrow said:

> '*It is not spirituality we are after for the young in any shape or form, but God himself. Spirituality is merely a help, a guide, a tool, a mentor, to drag us and them, to cajole us, to direct us, to tempt us to God. It is a mirror, a diamond, to help us reflect and reveal the nature of God. It is God we are after . . . Spirituality can't do things to us. It can only assist God to do them.*'

4.25   Nevertheless we welcome the growing awareness of the need, the desperate need, to help children and adults to learn the skills of prayer, to cope with silence and meditation, to grow in their capacity for prayer, to use music and singing to create and sustain concentration and attention. We are very conscious that our worship has become both wordy and possibly over-concerned with the need to hold children's attention by ceaseless activity. Yet, when one all-age confirmation group was told that the week's activities had left no time for the usual silent circle round the candle, the younger members were indignant and would not leave without their time of meditation. One parish priest at the Family Communion calls for a specific moment of silence before the distribution and all ages, including the children and helpers in the children's corner, are united in that special moment of stillness. We are also aware of children's and adults' growing spirituality in all sorts of groups: Saturday morning meditation groups, prayer groups, Bible study groups and so on. We look for those within the Church who are skilful in the realm of spirituality to share those gifts with children's leaders and, through them, with the children.

WORSHIP

4.26   Particular worship events can move, refresh, stimulate, feed or give insight. They are important and often formative experiences, no less for children as for adults. Worship is an integral part of the life of faith, in which the children, part of the faith community, rightly participate. They too may experience the transcendent, find directions for thoughts and feelings and share the cycle of festivals. Small children know instinctively and easily that worship is for them (as everything is) but, as they grow older, soon notice if they are being excluded or demoted by the language, by enforced inaction, by non-participation at the Communion or if their concerns and experiences have no part to play.

4.27   As our Survey shows, the non-Eucharistic 'Family Services' play a significant part in the pattern of worship in many parishes. However our Survey also shows that their congregations, and therefore their character, vary considerably. There are Services with 300 adults and 200 children, but also Services with 23 adults and five children, or 16 adults and no children! We note the comment from one incumbent that

'in practice very few, if any, attend a monthly Family Service',
or of another that

'no extra people attend and slightly less children participate than usual'
and contrast this with parishes like the one where the average attendance at the Sunday morning service is 27 but rises at the monthly 'Family Service' to 107, with more children than adults. These examples suggest that a careful assessment needs to be made of the effectiveness of such services in different situations, and of the varying needs for resources for those arranging them. We have already noted difficulties about the term 'Family' (3.14-3.21), and suggest that PCCs should think carefully about the name used for these services.

4.28   The continued success of such services in some parishes suggests some important factors in our thinking. The attempt to involve children in worship and learning with their families - parent or parents, and other adult members of the congregation - has obviously paid dividends in some situations. If this activity of worship is as important as we think it is, many parents do want to share in it with their children. Moreover, they frequently find the teaching aimed at their children more comprehensible than the normal sermon. 'Family Services' have been sufficiently flexible to accommodate those who come without any member of their family, and can meet the needs of a wide age range.

4.29   In some parishes, however, they have not overcome some significant limitations. Such a service has not always been a successful bridge for adults or children into other, for example, eucharistic services. It has not always escaped the charge of creating two congregations. It has not necessarily provided the depth of diet for either the children or the adults. It is as difficult to believe that a monthly Family Service is sufficient Christian nurture for a child as that a weekly sermon is so for an adult. Both need more. We welcome the development of Worship Advisory Groups in some dioceses and hope that they, with the Board of Education and the Liturgical Commission, will give attention to these services, and to Communion Services where children are present. In particular, we await with interest the suggestions of the Liturgical Commission working party presently examining these services.

4.30   Growing in faith also involves growing in worship. If adults can, by their example, help children to learn the skills of worship - silence and concentration, the use of symbol and ritual, the practice of prayer - then the children can also bring their own particular capacities for worship - singing the offertory, providing artwork for an altar frontal, adding drama to the ministry of the Word, writing prayers, giving expression to the creed, dancing their thanksgiving. To assist the wider congregation, the Church has a crying need to learn more about worship which draws the community, and the concerns and talents of all its members, together.

4.31   For many parishes the central service on Sunday is the Holy Communion Service. We have just seen how the children can contribute to the richness of worship and feel part of this fellowship. In some parishes the children are made to feel very much part of the Communion service. It is a common practice for them to spend some time in their peer groups, joining the adults at the Peace or the offertory. Often the children are encouraged to share a song or pictures or some drama with the adults, or to bring up their models or banners in the offertory procession. Even more important are the signs of welcome which they are given by the members of the congregation. Nevertheless they are excluded from the central act of the service. In this sense they are not 'members together of the body of Christ'. For some parishes this has become a real and urgent pastoral issue, and many diocesan Advisers are conscious of a growing demand for children to be admitted to Communion, or at least for a decision about the issue. Here is the experience of one local ecumenical project (Anglican/URC/Methodist):

> 'At Communion people stand in a circle (or concentric circles if there are a lot), and administer to each other round the circle. So the presence of children was really a challenge, since it was "me" who had to refuse, not just a priest the other side of an altar rail. And because children feel free to speak, and are listened to, the issue became real. So there was the initial meeting. Then two Sunday worship sessions were structured to talk about it and both adults and children studied the Bible passages and contributed to the discussion.'

4.32   General Synod received the Report *Communion before Confirmation?* in 1985. We have not thought it appropriate to repeat the arguments here, but we suggest that this is an urgent matter for the Church to resolve, bound up as it is with the wider issue of the status of children and their place in the Church.

4.33   It has been impossible to do more than point out potential growth areas, taking into account some of the consequences of the way faith grows and taking seriously the pilgrim model of the Church. We believe that these areas, concentrating as they do on children and adults growing together in faith in Church and home, should receive more attention and resources, to the benefit of children in the way. We are aware that this places a heavy demand on Church teachers and leaders; nevertheless, we look forward to a gradual transformation of the way we think about children in the Church.

JAMES FOWLER'S STAGES OF FAITH

(Primal Faith, sometimes included by Fowler as Stage 1)
1 Intuitive-Projective Faith
2 Mythic-Literal Faith
3 Synthetic-Conventional Faith
4 Individuative-Reflective Faith
5 Paradoxical-Consolidative Faith (now called Conjunctive Faith by Fowler)
6 Universalising Faith

The child moves from the dependence and trust on parents as super-ordinate power and wisdom [primal faith] to the wider experience of sharing in stories, symbols and rituals. These enrich the understanding and provide powerful identification and aspiration, guidance and reassurance as he or she endeavours to understand the world and give it unity and sense [Stage 1 - intuitive-projective faith]. From this she or he moves to rely on stories, rules, and the implicit values of the family's faith experience. Stories, practices and the family's beliefs are valued but in a concrete and literal sense. She or he is secure in this, but unable to find an overall direction and meaning from the component parts [Stage 2 - mythic-literal faith]. Next he or she moves to search for 'a story of my stories', a sense of the meaning of life generally, and of meaning and purpose in his or her own life in particular. The elements which make up this personal and original faith system is compiled of conventional elements, to be subjected to self-critical reflection and enquiry [Stage 3 - synthetic-conventional faith]. Later the person moves to Stage 4 [individuative-reflective faith] which is more personally chosen and believed, with an awareness that his or her views are different from that of some other people, and able to be expressed in abstract terms. In Stage 5 [paradoxical-consolidative] many different ideas and perspectives, suppressed or evaded before, are worked at, contradictions and tensions held in balance and apparently simple propositional statements reached. Stage 6 [universalising] is the final stage, typical of saints, where coherence gives a new simplicity centred on 'a oneness beyond but inclusive of the manyness of Being'!

RECOMMENDATIONS

1 The Board of Education should commission an appraisal of the research into faith development and its implications for Christian nurture.

Further research is required into the critical stages of transition and growth in a child's spiritual development, and the appropriate support to be offered by the Church to parents and children at these times.

2 A resolution of the issue of Communion before Confirmation is required as a matter of urgency.

3 The Board of Education and the Liturgical Commission should examine the need for new liturgies to serve all-age worship, and in particular for a form of Eucharist suitable for when children are present. There should be full consultation with leaders and parents of young children.

4 Funding should be sought for a field officer, responsible to the Board of Education, to promote experiments, produce resources and disseminate information relating to all-age learning.

5. Leadership Worthy of the Children

LEADERSHIP IN THE PARISHES

'I don't remember what I was taught. But I do remember some of the people who taught me.'

5.1 One of our major concerns in looking at the place of children within our Church today is to encourage PCCs, parish education committees and leaders of children's groups to re-examine the appropriateness of their styles of work with children and families, and to re-assess, where necessary, the priorities which they set themselves. Equally important is to look at their methods of outreach to children outside the Church or on the edge of it. The quality of leadership needed to implement their decision is obviously of paramount importance.

5.2 This may appear to suggest dissatisfaction with the present leadership in our parishes. This is only a partial truth. We would want, and we would like the whole Church with us, to pay tribute to those thousands of individuals who week by week, with great dedication and commitment, work with children in the Church. For far too long and in far too many places they have been unsung and unsupported in this essential aspect of the life of the Christian fellowship. But the greatest dissatisfaction with the leadership we offer comes from many of the leaders themselves, who are profoundly aware that they need additional skills, support and resources for the tasks they are given. We therefore make no apology for exploring this in greater detail for each of the different contexts of leadership we have identified.

5.3 What are the new elements of leadership identified in our understanding of the place of children in the Church? We need leaders who recognise that children, and adults, grow and develop in faith through what they share in worship and what they experience together in Christian fellowship as much as through what they are taught. We need leaders who recognise and accept that they do not have all to give and the children all to receive; who recognise and accept that their leadership must be gladly and appropriately shared with the incumbent, with other members of the congregation, with parents and, in particular circumstances, with the children themselves. We need leaders who recognise and accept that once they themselves cease to grow in their Christian life and understanding, once they regard themselves as having arrived while the children are still on the road, once they stop sharing themselves with the children, their usefulness is dramatically diminished.

We would make a special plea for the recruitment of more male leaders. Boys need models of Christian men, and a proper balance of men and women is important to all the children.

We recognise that there will continue to be different ways of working with children in church, and that for some parishes there may be many steps on the way to a more integrated approach. But, because it is a new concept for many people, we examine first the leadership for all-age activities.

LEADING ALL-AGE LEARNING ACTIVITIES AND WORSHIP

'Church is good because adults are with you and show you what to do.'

5.4   The qualities we have identified above cover every aspect of our work with children. However, they are particularly relevant to all-age activity. In this context there is an additional requirement. Leaders must genuinely believe that *all* are learners and fellow-worshippers and have the ability to convince others – adults and children – that this is and can be so. For many leaders the pattern of hived-off age or interest groups may be so ingrained that the possibility of alternatives is difficult, if not impossible, to contemplate, and they will need help to understand and, if possible, experience what is being envisaged. Some description of all-age activities, like those in 4.15 to 4.18 of this Report, will help, as will visits to other churches which are involved in such work. The mutual support of a deanery event to try out the ideas on a one-off, or more regular, basis could be particularly beneficial. Certainly the implementation of planned learning activities, whether on a regular or an occasional basis, has a better prospect of success when a *group* works together to plan them.

5.5 In many parishes this will be undertaken by the education committee, of which the incumbent will almost certainly be a member, though not necessarily the chairman. In others a special planning group will be created for each event or series of sessions. Because this group or committee will need to look at the theological basis for their programme, as well as to work out its content and the methods to be used, this group will need to include someone with theological understanding. It will also need people to represent the different ages and experiences of the proposed participants, and people who understand the way in which it is possible to learn through creative activities. It would be good to see young people and children taking part in this planning (in itself a valuable learning experience) and sharing skills in the actual programme.

5.6 The work of the group will need to be facilitated by the skills of a good chairperson: someone who can keep the group to its task and encourage the participation of each member, and who can check everyone's agreement to, and understanding of, the decisions made. He or she may need to impart factual information, take responsibility for the running of the group and suggest ways forward, but will also need to learn from the other members and share with them in mutual learning experiences as they try out ideas in preparation for the programme itself. It is important to note that leadership here may have more to do with co-ordinating a group of adults than with being face-to-face with a group of children. Many dioceses and organisations provide courses where such leadership skills can be learned and practised, and the courses of the Regional Churches' Training Groups are particularly recommended.

5.7 The importance of careful planning and theological reflection, which are necessities for any learning event catering for different ages, is one of the new lessons we are learning from this type of venture. It has also demonstrated what leaders have always known, but not always followed: that they cannot represent in their own person all the skills necessary for successful learning.

5.8 All-age learning will also depend upon helping forward those whose particular skills within a congregation can be used and shared to enrich the life of the whole. Parishes need to look outside the congregation for additional skills and resources; this can be a particularly valuable way of bringing newcomers into contact with the life of the congregation. An art teacher or carpenter does not need to be a worshipping Christian in order to encourage a group to produce a piece of practical work. But they will need to be clearly briefed, and helped to see that many activities suitable for all ages to share, while being important in their own right, are also designed to encourage people to talk and exchange experiences and insights. Christian adults working with the children, and Christian children working with adults, will themselves provide the Christian content and context.

One all-age group which made a collage of 'Belonging to the Church' not only had the satisfaction of working together and producing a finished collage; chatting as they worked, they also learned from one another about the groups inside and outside the Church to which they belonged, and discovered how each one of them 'fitted' into the Church itself. Both the 'expert' who explained how to make a collage and the members of the group were made aware of the importance of this conversation; they also discovered the power of communication which a visual presentation may possess.

The expert and other adults may need help to see how the gifts of the children can be most appropriately involved in an activity and the children's insights related to those of other members.

5.9   For everyone, therefore, involved in learning together the skills of communicating and listening are important, and everyone is both learner and leader. The children need the experience and wisdom of the adults. The adults need to learn from the children, who can lead them into enriching experiences and enjoyable skills. Are we to deny adults the insights of children? Dare we impoverish our own growth and continue to arrange for children to 'learn' in isolation from the rest of the Christian family? *The Child in the Church* report said,

> 'The Church that does not accept children unconditionally into its fellowship is depriving those children of what is rightfully theirs, but the deprivation such as the Church itself will suffer is far more grave.'

5.10   Many adults have stayed with a childish faith and a childish view of God. The children can help us to return to the childlike experience of seeking after knowledge, of questioning, of the expectation of a continuing growth of understanding, of a capacity for awe and wonder, of an expectancy that life will reveal things of beauty, of an affinity with the spiritual, but with an awareness of the complexity of life lived at the end of the twentieth century.

5.11 Our concern so far has been for the leadership of all-age learning events of a fairly structured kind. For many Christian adults their learning takes place less formally, in house-groups where they share in Bible study, discussion and prayer. Children too respond to small familiar groups. They become confident and able to contribute, so learning and helping others to learn in such groups. Is there a place for house-groups which include children, and should our house-group leaders be helped to envisage and facilitate their membership? The skills and techniques which these leaders use in encouraging adult members to participate would be effective for the children also, and careful checking out that everyone, including the children, understands what is said could be beneficial to the whole group. In one parish a group meets regularly to discuss and plan the work being done in various house-groups in the parish, to look at books and discussion material and the overall composition of the groups, and to share in training the group leaders.

5.12 Planning all-age worship is another area needing our consideration. Some clergy and some lay leaders have gifts which make them especially good at leading services for people of all ages, particularly for those who are fairly new to worship. The danger may be that success depends on that one person's 'charisma' and falters when he or she is not available. Many leaders of such services, however, find it difficult to sustain ideas week after week, or month after month. They worry about maintaining the balance between liturgical and non-liturgical worship, between teaching and worship, between using novel and familiar patterns and ideas.

In one parish a group of lay people share with the priest in the preparation of the Sunday Eucharist, choosing the intercessions, thinking and talking about the liturgy, the Church calendar and the themes for the Sunday, and bearing in mind the children and the newcomers who will be present.

5.13 In other parishes, a similar group prepares the non-liturgical services, choosing themes, co-ordinating with the learning activities of the various groups and clubs, and organising their involvement in readings, drama, music and so on.

5.14 The model for the leader is that of the fellow traveller on the Emmaus Road, who shared his faith and experience and understanding - only afterwards did the travellers realise that their hearts had burned within them. The biblical evidence of the development of many of the disciples into leaders is one worthy of our study and consideration. The leaders that our children need and deserve are fellow pilgrims who will walk with them for part of their journey, but who have insights and experience to share and will respond to the child's immediate needs. This demands that every congregation be involved in the whole process of Christian education and see themselves as leaders of those young in years, or young in the faith.

5.15 Parishes who find these ideas of all-age learning and worshipping together new and difficult to envisage or plan will need to look elsewhere for advice and ideas – to diocesan Children's Work Advisers and Adult Advisers, for example. Visits to similar programmes and services in other parishes or churches are helpful and to be encouraged. The use of the deanery, or the local Council of Churches, as a natural and readily available group of Churches for sharing all-age events and exchange visits has proved useful in many dioceses, and has led to a wider exchange of resources, ideas and experiences. Many diocesan Advisers and Mothers' Union committees organise family or all-age events in dioceses and deaneries. Some dioceses have held all-age days in the cathedral, involving large numbers of people in group work, worship and fellowship together. Sometimes diocesan resource centres are used as venues for parish groups to meet together, to use and discover resources, to try out activities for themselves and to receive advice from the staff if required. There already exist a number of ways in which planning groups and leaders can find help in these enterprises.

LEADING CHILDREN'S GROUPS – IN THE CHURCH

'Children today have everything the video can offer, and repeats all Sunday morning. Yet they are still presented in Sunday School with "the crayon tin", the baby stools, and long-haired Jesus in his nightie.' (From an article by Susanne Garnett in *Christian* magazine, July/August 1987.)

5.16 Some parishes will decide to move completely to a new pattern of all-age learning. Some parishes will arrange the occasional all-age event. Some will try to find ways of involving children more clearly in worship and other Church activities. Some will be more concerned to reach out to children outside the Church. In almost all parishes some children's groups will continue to be appropriate. There may, therefore, be a crèche or an under-fives group on Sundays, a Sunday club or group meeting for children during part of the worship time, a weekday club for children belonging to one church or for those outside it, a holiday club, and so on. What do the leaders of such groups chiefly bring to the children who come under their influence? It cannot be said often enough that what is needed is not primarily an expert interpreter of some course material, or even a charismatic presence in worship, but above all a potent model for the children of a Christian adult, with all the responsibility and opportunity that that involves. This adult needs to be aware of the actual 'world' of children, and to be realistic about their attitudes and interests, their problems and their joys. Not a saint, but a person who is on the same pilgrimage of faith, in the way of Christ, who brings to his or her understanding of faith at least the same depth of study, enquiry and willingness to learn as he or she brings to any other consuming interest in his or her life. These adults may be with the children week by week throughout the year, or may work on a rota system, or in teams responsible for particular projects.

The incumbent and the PCC need to ensure that there is adequate support for them, and also that their own spiritual lives are not allowed to suffer. The adult who is out of touch with the worshipping, learning, sacramental life of the Church will be deprived of spiritual nourishment, and can become ineffective in providing opportunities for spiritual development for the children. The children may encourage and inspire the adults, of course, but this may not be sufficient if they are all to grow to spiritual maturity.

5.17 The PCC needs to ensure that the interests of the children are represented. Sometimes the man or woman who has regular contact with the children will also represent their interests to the wider congregation, but this need not necessarily be the best model. For example, a PCC or committee member can be designated who will make sure that the children are remembered when parish events are planned; someone who can ensure that the children are not put into separate groups unnecessarily, but who understands children and can see that separate arrangements are made for them when really appropriate; someone to see that the budget includes a reasonable amount for the development of all-age and children's work; someone who will see that the children's contribution to the life of the parish is not overlooked nor the needs of children outside the Church life neglected. At the same time, a deliberate policy of support for the leaders of groups needs to be planned. So often the provision for children's concerns is overlooked through negligence rather than intention.

5.18 Almost all dioceses offer training courses for leaders of children's groups. Some, like the Truro scheme, which is based on distance learning and tutorial techniques, takes up to two years to complete and leads to a Bishop's Certificate. Other dioceses tailor courses to fit the particular circumstances of a parish or deanery; some offer training which is inter-denominational. It is time that many training schemes were re-assessed and re-structured to take account of new trends. Some fundamental questions suggest themselves. Do the skills, knowledge, processes you seek to impart match the needs of (a) the leader, (b) the children, (c) the congregational life of our parishes? Do they sufficiently take into account the circumstances in which our children are brought up, educated, influenced? Do they really gear children to think as Christians about the different aspects of their lives and to become Christian adults? Honest answers to these questions will suggest the need for new elements and new emphases in our training courses.

5.19 Courses need, for example, to include training in creative listening skills. Listening is a much more difficult task than most people imagine. To give full attention to what another person is saying, without at the same time distracting one's own attention by assessing their views and framing a reply, requires both skill and practice. Really to hear what a child is saying is often even more difficult. Our Report has discussed the importance of providing the best environment for the growth of spirituality in children. A course, therefore, needs to include a consideration of the components of spirituality and the potential and actual spirituality of the child, together with help for the spiritual development of the leader.

Whether working with children or with all ages, a major part of the leader's task is to enable other people to contribute their thinking and their skills to the whole group. An examination of this role also needs to be a component of a training course, together with a grasp of the principles and practice of group behaviour and group work.

Leaders also need to examine faith development theory, relating it to their knowledge of the children in their care. It is also essential that they are enabled to think through their own journey of faith and to identify the factors which assist them in their own search for meaning and truth. Learning is a complex process, so leaders need to understand how effective learning takes place. A variety of learning styles should be examined and a chance given to explore the appropriateness of different methods for different purposes and situations. Training courses should be experiential rather than didactic in style and leaders should be given opportunities to relate their learning to the situations in which they work.

The demands that we should be making on leaders of all-age and children's groups are great. They should be matched by the provision and expectation of adequate training. There is an urgent need for work to be done in developing new training schemes. There is also a concern that there should be adequate provision of diocesan staff members to initiate and sustain training.

If these leaders in the Church are not thought worthy of support, interest and concern by their fellow worshipping Christians, but only as those who so splendidly remove the children so that the real business of worship can proceed quietly, then we devalue not only the leaders and the children, but also the adults who are fellow-Christians in the way of faith.

LEADING OUTREACH GROUPS

5.20   Though most parishes would affirm the need to evangelise children and families in their communities, many are discouraged by the complexity of the task and the difficulty of finding willing and competent leaders. We would not wish to minimise the difficulties, but would suggest that the first hurdle is over when the precise nature of a task is identified (as we have seen in chapter 2). An evangelistic mission is usually headed-up by people from outside the parish, assisted by parishioners whom they train in visiting, group leadership and communication skills. A long-term club or group set up as an evangelistic enterprise in a parish needs equally skilled and sensitive leadership. Help should be sought from diocesan missioners, children's Advisers and skilled evangelists.

5.21   What are the special elements of leadership required from those who are to work with children and families outside the familiar context of Church life? Potential leaders need to recognise that those they seek to reach are outside churchy conventions and will bring little, if any, awareness or recognition of Christian assumptions. The children involved will often have little, if any, parental support. In fact a potential for real disharmony exists between the leaders' values and assumptions, however tactfully expressed, and those of the home. Leaders working through this issue will need considerable support and guidance. Often it will be the isolation and 'one-ness' of leadership that strikes them most forcibly because many of the fixed points of school, home or church will not apply. And leaders, however experienced, will find it difficult to appreciate that in these contexts there is often no room at all for the preaching and moralising into which we slip, usually unconsciously, in more formal groups.

5.22   Where a parish's aim is to concentrate more on outreach work through serving the community, the issue of leadership is equally important. Of course, the leader needs the particular skills called for by this type of outreach work: those of, for example, the playgroup leader. Some tasks, like that of counselling, are highly skilled. They should only be undertaken by those who have been properly trained. In addition, the parish is asking that leaders will have a clear grasp of what it means to proclaim the gospel through actions rather than words, showing the power of Christ in their character and behaviour rather than in direct challenge to commitment. They may need to recognise that offering direct teaching on Christian faith to some individuals may be the least helpful thing to do at that moment, and may be counter-productive. Leaders need sensitivity and integrity, and an understanding of their own continuing journey of faith.

5.23   In setting up a children's club, for example, the task is to match the needs and interests of the youngsters with the interests and skills of potential leaders, and to look for leaders who can fulfil particular roles. Some work best in a structured programme, others in a more informal situation.

> 'It's for under-eights and it's called Cru-club. It happens on Thursdays. The children begin to arrive at 3.40 p.m., hang their coats in the garage and come straight into the kitchen where they are given squash and a biscuit. In the hall they find their name card and put it on the attendance chart. New children are welcomed; name, address and birthday recorded. Then they are taken into the sitting room where some quiet activity is in progress. At 4 p.m. we start our worship time. Later we spread all over the house, into bedrooms as well as hall and dining room. Our programme consists of games, stories, singing and prayer-time.'

5.24   We can see how this kind of group might attract friends of church children as well as those already in touch with the church. In another parish, a similar group in a home had a less structured programme which provided opportunity for chat and doing things together. The only 'Christian' or 'religious talk' was that raised by the children themselves. Very slowly some links were made with the church, but only after careful and sensitive consultation with the children. There was no pressure on those who did not wish to join in. The children came because of the open, welcoming, caring attitude of the leader.

5.25   Such leaders need the most careful support from the Church, and help to make sure that the club stays within reasonable limits in its use of the family house, the time and the helpers available. It is all too easy to leave a leader to get on with a successful venture, and give no further thought or assistance. Those offering to lead such groups, as well as those leading parent and toddler groups, playgroups, shopping crèches and the like, need to be put in touch with those who can offer relevant advice and training - the Mothers' Union, the Pre-School Playgroup Association, diocesan Advisers or Family Life workers, for example. The PCC can play its part too by encouraging training, by giving practical help and resources and, above all, by maintaining an awareness of, and an interest in, what they are doing.

PARENTS AS LEADERS

'Mum, when will I be old enough to stay at home from church, and clean the car with Daddy?'

5.26   No matter how good the provisions of the local church are for the Christian nurture of the children with whom it has contact, its influence can be negated by the influence of the home. A child who does not go to playgroup or nursery school will probably spend at least 21,900 working hours within the home. It could take the average church group more than 421 years to spend the same amount of time with the child. Even then it would not be equally influential! The earliest experiences of life are particularly important. Basic attitudes and assumptions will have been formed by the time the child goes to school. Even though that person may later consciously reject those attitudes, their influence will remain. The first models which a child has are its parents. Their attitudes as well as their actions will be copied, and foundations of trust and security need to be laid by them.

5.27 One of the key lessons which we all need to learn from faith development and other work on the spiritual growth of children is the central influence of parents. This is as true about faith as about every other aspect of a child's development. All those qualities which will enable a child to enter into the processes of faith - the responsibilities of moral thinking, the self-discipline of loving relationships - are rooted in the child's early experience. We are only just beginning to see how important it is to help parents to nurture their child's capacity to respond to the world of mystery, wonder and imagination. We already know that self-esteem and the capacity to enter into caring, loving relationships will flow from early family life, yet we are too diffident or too uncertain to know how best to counsel even Christian families in these matters. There is a long way to go, both centrally and in dioceses, before we can feel confident about offering the sort of realistic support and guidance to which families will respond.

5.28 If parishes take this seriously, those containing young families need to look carefully at their programmes and provisions. One church has made a deliberate decision to ensure that no parents are unable to come to worship or gatherings because the baby is ill or the toddler behaving badly. There is a list of church members prepared to baby-sit; this is recognised as a Christian ministry and no payment is accepted. Indeed, it has led to a furthering of friendship in the Church.

5.29 It would be salutary to look at the events in the parish over one month and see how many activities support and affirm family life, and how many militate against it. How often are parents encouraged to be away from their children? What opportunities are there for the family to be together at church events? What space is left for the family to follow its own interests?

5.30 More directly, we need to ask what help is given to parents to assist them in their task of being Christian parents. Many would welcome a group where they and their children could share with other families their questions, their seeking, their experiences and their desire to learn about their faith. In one parish parents of the tiny children who use the crèche are doing exactly this. They meet together weekly and share their ideas, thoughts and needs. Sometimes their clergy join them; sometimes another member of the congregation who has grown-up children, or a member of the choir, or Mothers'

Union, or other group talks with them. There are opportunities to talk about the problems and expectations raised by bringing children to church, the thoughts of others in the congregation about their presence, as well as about questions of faith and practice. They and their children are building a fellowship with each other and with others in the worshipping congregation.

5.31 Some parishes, particularly some Roman Catholic parishes in the USA, have formed 'family cluster groups' where parents and children from several families meet regularly to explore Christian themes together, through discussion, worship, practical activities and shared meals. The Church of England needs to try out such methods by which parents are helped to lead and learn with their children in the way of faith. Individual families who are too self-conscious to learn together by themselves in any regular pattern may find it easier to co-operate with other families in this way, meeting perhaps on a Saturday evening and following a simple scheme for activities, stories and praying together.

5.32 Many Christian parents would also welcome ideas for informal simple rituals which would remind the family of its Christian faith and practice. We welcome the proposed production of such a book of resources by Church House Publishing, and would suggest the need for parents to share with one another their own ideas and practices. Parents can also be helped by suggestions and activities which spill over from the Pram Service or the Sunday service: a model to be finished and brought back, or a candle to be taken and used at home, for example. Other Christian families want to engage in family prayers and Bible reading on a daily or weekly basis. The parish and the diocese could encourage them by drawing their attention to suitable books or schemes, and by the occasional meeting to advise on what works. In many churches a well-run bookstall displays recent books and resources which parents and children will find helpful. Other churches have a flourishing lending library for the same purpose.

Many parents want to share their faith with their children; others would like to discover faith with their children, and may lack the confidence to begin. The Church has a responsibility to support and help them.

5.33 Perhaps that help should begin in marriage preparation, when the joys and responsibilities of parenthood can be discussed as part of the expected changing pattern of married life. One parish arranges for a group of young and older parents to meet together so that they can share their common concern about bringing up children in Christian homes in a world in which (as we saw in our first chapter) many forces and pressures strive to claim them.

Particular difficulties and conflicts are bound to occur for a parent whose partner is apathetic or opposed to the Christian faith and/or to churchgoing. In seeking to help them we must not enforce extra tensions and stress on them. Informal visiting at a convenient time, or invitations to 'come when you can' to a group, are likely to be more helpful than pressure to attend every week yet another group or activity. Thought as to occasions when both partners can be invited to a social occasion (genuinely without strings) would be sensible, and the support of a baby-sitting offer may also be helpful. Leaders of children's groups may well be in this situation, and again care needs to be taken not to place unbearable or damaging demands upon them.

5.34   Often parents need and want help, not specifically with the Christian upbringing of their children, but with parenting skills. The experiences and skills of members of the congregation could be very appropriate here, when their own parents and family may be some distance away. Parents with young children often need advice and reassurance about dealing with sleeplessness or 'naughtiness'; the parents of teenagers need to talk about the problems of discipline or their concerns about influences and pressures on their children, and so on. The local church is one community which can arrange for groups of parents to talk over their concerns, with or without 'experts'. One church reports as one of the most useful activities of its life a group of parents who met each week for six weeks to share experiences. Other parishes have laid on more structured courses on parenting. The work of Micki and Terri Quinn is a useful resource for this kind of group (see Book List, page 97). Certainly many parents have been seen to respond to these initiatives, and parents from outside as well as inside the Church have availed themselves of the opportunities provided.

5.35   One parish arranged a house-group for parents whose children had been baptised within the last six months. Eight couples were invited to take part. Four couples accepted. The aim was laid out before the meeting: to meet together, share experiences of living with babies and young children, and look at the question, 'What does it mean, or not mean, for all of us to be part of God's family?' The evening proved so successful that they arranged another meeting, at the home of one of the other 'baptism couples', and in all had six meetings.

LEADERSHIP BY THE CLERGY

'I think the vicar does preaches, he wears a long cloak and he likes to read books and believes in God and vicars help children and old and young people.'

5.36   The vicar does all these things and more! We are not necessarily asking clergy to do yet more things – but we are suggesting a new way of looking at what is done. We are asking them to lead their parishes into what may be a new vision and understanding of the place of children in the Church. We are suggesting that children are on the same journey of faith as the adults in the Church. They are all in the way of faith. They all need to grow in understanding of their faith, in closeness to God and in awareness of his purposes. However far a parish can go in implementing new ways of working, or however tentative changes need to be, the outdated ideas of children being isolated in their worship and learning, seen as only recipients of adult knowledge, must be left behind. Work with children must be integrated into the journey of faith of the whole parish; the needs of children and families outside the Church must also be taken seriously.

5.37   For some clergy, then, a new approach to Christian nurture and mission may be necessary. For all clergy, we ask that they encourage their PCCs and congregations to look at the principles underlying their work and the provisions made. Suggestions for such discussions are provided on page 93 and in the video material which has been produced to promote discussion of the main ideas of this Report (see page 97).

5.38   Once the aims and objectives of the parish have been set we would expect that an education committee or special planning group would implement the decisions. The incumbent and the PCC will, of course, ultimately be responsible for the nurture in the parish, together with its programme of outreach. They should receive regular reports of the work and ensure that adequate support is provided. Many clergy need help in finding ways to enable lay people to use their gifts. The growing emphasis on lay involvement and participation, and the consideration of parochial resources, of skills and expertise, of time and talents, all suggest that in some ways the process has started.

CLERGY TRAINING

5.39   In order to enthuse leaders in the parish, clergy need to be aware of the needs of children and families, and to be ready to listen to those who have that knowledge, including children and parents wherever possible. We recognise the already full programme of theological colleges, post-ordination and in-service training. Nevertheless, we would recommend that they should include learning about children, parenting skills, educational psychology, learning styles, group behaviour, models for Christian nurture, evangelism and mission to children and families, and resources for work with children, families and all ages in the Church. Indeed, we suggest that understanding children and children's learning will also assist their understanding of adults and adult learning.

Not all clergy will feel themselves to be particularly competent or gifted at working with children, nor are we suggesting that they all should be. They should be encouraged to delegate where necessary. They do, however, need to understand what is happening and be ready to stimulate thinking about it. Above all, they need themselves to have taken part in learning through experiential methods, and in using creative, imaginative activities. For many clergy, their own training and education has been entirely through didactic and tutorial methods. The balance needs to be redressed in ordination, post-ordination and in-service training if they are to understand more fully how people of different ages and stages can learn together and from one another. Much of this would also apply to the training of Readers. Diocesan education staff should be involved in such training sessions. There is also in many dioceses and deaneries a need to identify people in a deanery with particular skills and experience who can help to plan and take part in training sessions for clergy and laity together.

DIOCESAN SUPPORT

5.40   A reconsideration of the question of leadership, and the involvement of the parish in the nurture both of its young and of people of every age, poses questions for diocesan education staff. The first need is for adequate staffing, but there is equally a need for co-ordination and planning between Adult, Youth and Children's

Advisers and Family Life Workers. There are implications here for General Synod, diocesan and parish budgets, for consideration of training needs and the provision of staff and resources. Any attempt to change attitudes and introduce new ways of working calls for extra time to be given to explaining, demonstrating and resourcing the new approaches. Parish groups will need to turn to Advisers who can work alongside them as they plan and then implement their ideas, and who can afterwards assist them to evaluate what has happened, and to build on their experiences.

RECOMMENDATIONS

1   Parishes should review the support they offer to those who lead their educational work, with particular reference to
    - realistic finance for resources,
    - regular training,
    - personal support and development.

2   Those responsible for ministerial training should review the adequacy of their consideration of children in the Church and society. The possibility of liaison with professionals in teacher training departments in universities and in higher and further education colleges should be considered.

3   The training of leaders for all-age learning should be explored by Diocesan Education Committees in conjunction with the recommendations about developing leadership in *Faith in the City* and the guidelines suggested in *Called to be Adult Disciples*.

4   Diocesan Education Councils should reassess their staff and resources in the light of the training and assistance which will need to be offered to parishes to implement the Recommendations in this Report.

6. A Biblical and Theological Reflection

'Sons are a heritage from the Lord,
children a reward from him.' (Psalm 127.3)

'Your wife will be like a fruitful vine
within your house;
your children will be like olive shoots
around your table.
Lo, thus shall the man be blessed
who fears the Lord.' (Psalm 128.3-4)

6.1   The Old Testament has a positive attitude to the birth of children, especially of sons. It was important to continue the family line and to have someone to inherit the property. Children were important not only for the small family unit, but for the wider community. There must always be Israelites to occupy the land and to worship God as the covenant people[1]. There are many examples of God intervening to ensure offspring, as in the case of Abraham and Sarah (Genesis 17.19), the Hebrews in Egypt (Exodus 1-2), and Hannah (I Samuel 1). The last example also illustrates Old Testament attitudes to childlessness, which was seen as a cause of great shame for a woman. The law of levirate marriage (Deuteronomy 25.5-10) provided for the nearest kinsman to marry the childless widow and raise children to perpetuate the dead husband's family. So children were significant, and their existence was seen as a sign of God's blessing.

6.2   However, children seem to have been little valued as persons in their own right. They were valued rather for their potential, as future adult members of the covenant community (boys) or as guardians of the family and bearers of the next generation (girls). There is no sentimentality about children in the Old Testament. They are not used as a model of innocence. On the contrary, they are included in warnings of judgment:

'Their infants will be dashed to pieces before their eyes;
their houses will be looted and their wives ravished.'
(Isaiah 13.16)

They are used as symbols of lack of wisdom and understanding:

'I will make boys their officials; mere children will
govern them.' (Isaiah 3.4)

'Woe to you, O land, when your king is a child, and your
princes feast in the morning!' (Ecclesiastes 10.16)

Children were not seen as having any contribution of their own to make to the life of the community until they reached the age of being able to keep the Law.

6.3   Such education as was provided was geared to this end. In the pre-exilic period at least, for the majority of Israelite children there were no schools. Children learned at home. Boys learned their fathers' trade; girls learned home-making skills. Religious learning took place at home, by participation in religious festivals and in the religious life of the family. The Old Testament explicitly commands fathers to teach their children the history of God's dealings with Israel:

'On that day tell your son, "I do this because of what the
Lord did for me when I came out of Egypt."' (Exodus 13.8)

In the later post-exilic period, with its greater emphasis on the written word, education in schools, in the Torah and the traditions of the rabbis, became more common. So too did a fondness for strict discipline (see Ecclesiasticus 30.9-12). All education had the same aim: that of producing trained members of the covenant community, familiar with the commands of the Law, and able to fulfil their social and religious obligations.

6.4   Jesus seems to have inherited the unsentimentality of this attitude towards children. The Jewish pattern described above would have been the childhood and education he himself experienced. The clear-sighted and realistic way in which Jesus viewed children has been decisively demonstrated by Hans-Ruedi Weber[2]. In Matthew 11.16-19 (= Luke 7.31-35), Jesus paints an unidealised picture of children at play. Behind the gospels' use of 'child' as a metaphor for receptivity in Mark 10.15 and parallels, lies Jesus' acceptance of children as persons who matter in their own right. Dr Weber points out [3]that in the

73

famous passage about Jesus and the children in Mark 10.13-16 Jesus says nothing about children's goodness or innocence, but speaks of them as those to whom God gives the Kingdom in an act of free generosity. (See also the parable of the labourers in the vineyard, Matthew 20.1-20, a parable about God's unreasonable generosity to those who have had no chance to earn it.) The evangelists have contextualized Jesus' teaching on children to suit their own ecclesiastical purposes; but in the teaching of Jesus itself, children are not, as in Jewish thought, those who are only taught and trained, but those from whom adults can also learn. They are those who are vulnerable, like the 'poor in spirit' to whom belongs the Kingdom (Matthew) or the economically poor (Luke), like Jesus himself. They are special to God, as were orphans in the Old Testament, as those who cannot take care of themselves and are therefore open to receive from God, not through any merit, but because they know no other way. Weber says:

> '...it is the relationship with Jesus which makes these children representatives[4] of God. As such they are our teachers. In their objective humility and need, they cry "mother", "father", "Abba", and they stretch out their empty hands. If we want to learn how to receive the Kingdom and how to become God's representatives, we must learn it from the child in our midst.'[5]

6.5   In this view of Jesus' attitude to children, they are not to be seen simply as objects of education, those who need to be brought and trained for adulthood before they achieve any real significance. Rather they are seen as patterns of discipleship, those who teach as well as learn. Against the background of the Jewish attitude described above, and the Graeco-Roman view of children as primarily those to be trained for their place in society, this is an innovation on Jesus' part which we need to take seriously. This lends theological support to the view expressed in the report (chapter 3) that the school model of the nurture of children in the Church is inadequate.

6.6   A different model examined in chapter 3 is that of the family, which certainly has a biblical warrant. Family kinship is an important theme in the book of Genesis, where the kinship of humankind is not limited to the nation of Israel, but is traced back to the beginning of creation. We have seen above, that for the people of the Old Testament, education was family centred. The New Testament also seems to treat children as parts of family units. It speaks of the conversion and baptism of households (see, for instance, I Corinthians

74

16.15 and 16.33) which may be presumed to include children.[6] Other mentions of children in the epistles assume that they were present in the meeting of the congregation with their parents. They are included in the 'household code' instructions for family life: for example,

'Children obey your parents in the Lord, for this is right.
"Honour your father and mother."' (Ephesians 6.1-2)

6.7   In the teaching of Jesus, the image of 'family' is used as the primary model for relationships in the eschatological community:

'Then he looked at those seated in a circle around him and said, "Here are my mother and my brothers! Whoever does God's will is my brother and sister and mother."' (Mark 3.34f)

'Another man, one of his disciples, said to him, "Lord, first let me go and bury my father." But Jesus told him, "Follow me, and let the dead bury their own dead."' (Matthew 8.21f)

This is not, however, to be taken as implying hostility towards responsibility within the natural family. (See Mark 7.10-13, where Jesus quotes the commandment 'Honour your father and mother'.)

6.8   In the epistles, the family image for the Church is included alongside others such as new Israel, royal priesthood, holy nation, flock of Christ, new Temple:

'Consequently, you are no longer foreigners and aliens, but fellow-citizens with God's people and members of God's household.' (Ephesians 2.19. See also Galatians 6.10)

'...You also, like living stones, are being built into a spiritual house to be a holy priesthood...' (I Peter 2.5)

6.9   But more often the Bible speaks of the wider community, of Israel or the Church. The model of Christian nurture favoured in this report is that of the pilgrim people.[7] This image combines the idea of learning together from one another with that of a journey, in which those of all ages are travelling together, helping one another along, telling stories of the past, and acquiring knowledge and skills for the future.

Despite the importance of the settlement of the land in the Old Testament, much Old Testament material looks back to the time the Israelites spent journeying in the wilderness as a time of closeness to God, of God's guidance and Israel's dependence.[8] It looks back to the Exodus as the beginning of the journey, the setting out through God's act of liberation, and beyond that to Abraham, whose covenant with

God was based on his willingness to set out on a journey into the unknown. An early Old Testament creed begins, 'A wandering Aramean was my father...' (Deuteronomy 26.5). Israel sees itself as a people on a journey, from slavery to the promised land of God's blessing. It was on the journey through the wilderness that Israel encountered God at Mount Sinai and was given the Law, the foundation of its national life. Looking back, Israel places its origins as a nation under God at a point on that journey.

The Old Testament documents were compiled long after Israel had ceased to be nomadic and become a political and national entity. Nevertheless, the importance of the journey is still emphasised. Prophets and psalmists describe God's future restoration of Israel in terms of a new Exodus, a new journey through the wilderness:

'I am the Lord your God, who brought you out of Egypt; I will make you live in tents again...' (Hosea 12.9)

'When you went out before your people, O God, when you marched through the wasteland...' (Psalm 68.7)

(See also Isaiah 40.3, 42.6, etc.) Deuteronomy 1.31 says of the desert wanderings:

'There you saw how the Lord your God carried you, as a father carries his son, all the way you went until you reached this place.'

It is on the journey that the pilgrim people discover their need of God and feel God's care.[9]

6.10   Journeys play a key part in the New Testament too. It is on the road to Jerusalem that Jesus teaches his disciples about a messiahship that involves suffering. On the road to Emmaus two disciples learn the truth of the Resurrection (Luke 24.13-35). On the road to Damascus Paul encounters the risen Christ (Acts 9.1-9). Much Christian spirituality has picked up this theme and used it to describe progress in the spiritual life, progress which may include the desert experience of need and vulnerability.

6.11   The people of Israel remembered their time as a pilgrim people and kept the tradition alive through their worship. And in that all members of the family were included, children as well as adults. The Passover festival in particular was, and is, an occasion of making effective in the present the memory of God's past act of liberation, and of looking to the future ('next year in Jerusalem'). Christian theology has often interpreted the saving work of Christ in terms of an Exodus act of liberation from sin and death, and part of Christian worship consists in remembering that past event[10], making it accessible in the present, and looking to Christ's coming again in the future. So the Church can be seen as the new Israel, the pilgrim community. All are then involved in learning along the way, adults and children alike. And as in the Old Testament community, that learning happens as much by experience and participation in worship as by direct teaching. What the pilgrim church needs to help it on its way are stories of the past to help map out the journey; common worship in which the living God is experienced; and a confidence in an unknown future.

6.12 This brings us back to Jesus and his attitude to children. He extended the traditional view of children as those who are to be moulded and taught, and offered them as those from whom we can also learn. Being the pilgrim people means that all are called to the journey, and all involved in the teaching and learning on the way.

6.13 This may be a threatening image for the Church to grasp. The Old Testament community recognised the time of wilderness wandering as one of fear and set-back as well as of progress. It is more comfortable to see the Church as a safe and settled family than as a community on the move. 'Freedom is a hard and difficult road.'[11] But if we can come to terms with it, this model can be a fruitful way of looking at the Church in the changing modern world and of structuring the Church's education and nurture of its members so that all share in the exploration of the journey:

> 'Blessed are those whose strength is in you,
> who have set their hearts on pilgrimage.
> As they pass through the Valley of Baca,
> they make it a place of springs;
> the autumn rains also cover it with pools.
> They go from strength to strength
> till each appears before God in Zion.' (Psalm 84.5-7)

NOTES

1 On the significance of the land, see for example *The Land*, W. Brueggemann (Fortress Press); *The Gospel and the Land*, W.D. Davies (University of California Press).

2   Jesus and the Children, Hans-Ruedi Weber (WCC, 1979).

3   op. cit. p.19

4   cf. Mark 9.37, where the phrase is reminiscent of apostolic commissioning (see Matthew 10.40).

5   op. cit. p.51
This applies also to other vulnerable groups: 'Those who are farthest from the centre of religious and political power, the slaves, the children, the Gentiles, the women, become the paradigm for true discipleship.' *In Memory of Her*, E Schussler Fiorenza (SCM 1983, p.323).

6   In favour of this view, see *A Case for Infant Baptism*, Colin Buchanan (Grove Books on Ministry and Worship no. 20, p.20f). See also *Infant Baptism in the First Four Centuries*, J. Jeremias.

7   With I Peter 2.5 quoted above, compare I Peter 2.9 'a chosen people, a holy nation' and I Peter 2.11 'aliens and strangers in the world'.

8   On this tension see *Theological Diversity and the Authority of the Old Testament*, J. Goldingay (Eerdmans 1987, pp.68-9, 85).

9   On the significance of the wilderness in the Old Testament, see *True God*, Kenneth Leech (Sheldon Press 1985, pp.27-38).

10 See for example ASB Rite A, Eucharistic Prayers 1 and 2: 'through him you have freed us from the slavery of sin...'

11 *A Map of the New Country*, Sara Maitland (Routledge and Kegan Paul 1983, p.190).

7. The Survey

7.1   The research project was initiated as a thoroughly collaborative venture by the General Synod Board of Education, the National Conference of Religious Education Advisers and Children's Work Officers, and the Culham College Institute for Church Related Education. Oversight of the research project was undertaken by a small management group, representing the three sponsoring bodies: Colin Alves and Marjorie Freeman (General Synod Board of Education), David Lankshear and Steven Pearce (Diocesan Advisers), Leslie Francis and John Gay (Culham College Institute). Funding for the research project was provided by All Saints' Educational Trust, the Foundation of St Matthias, the Hockerill Educational Foundation, St Gabriel's Trust, the Sarum St Michael Educational Charity, St Christopher's Trust and the Central Church Fund of the Church of England. The administration of the research project was undertaken from the Culham College Institute by Leslie Francis, John Gay, David Lankshear, Elizabeth More O'Ferrall and Helen Piper.

7.2   The intention of the research project was to send a detailed questionnaire to every church or habitual place of worship within a certain number of dioceses. The questionnaire was developed from the survey instrument used by Leslie Francis in *Rural Anglicanism: a future for young Christians?* (Collins Liturgical Publications, 1985). The three parts of this questionnaire examine key background information about the churches, membership and participation in a range of activities, and a careful log of services and activities over an eight-day period from Sunday to Sunday.

THE RESPONSE

7.3   The research project began in February 1986 throughout 19 dioceses: Bath and Wells, Birmingham, Blackburn, Bristol, Carlisle, Chelmsford, Chester, Chichester, Derby, Durham, Gloucester, Lichfield, London, Peterborough, St Albans, Southwell, Truro, Worcester and York. Subsequently five other dioceses and one archdeaconry joined in the survey: Ely, Hereford, Oxford, Salisbury, Sheffield and the Isle of Wight.

‘7.4   In most cases the questionnaires were originally distributed by the diocesan Advisers. After a period of time reminder requests were mailed from the Culham College Institute. All told, questionnaires were sent to 9,914 churches or worship centres. By the end of July 1987, 6,921 replies had been received, representing a 70 per cent response rate. The responses vary considerably from diocese to diocese, as indicated by Table 1. (See page 89.) The authors of the research project are immensely grateful to the diocesan Advisers and the many clergy and lay people who have given generously of their time in completing and returning the questionnaires. A number of parishes have told us that they have found completing the questionnaire a very helpful way of reflecting on what they are doing.

7.5   What has emerged from this survey is one of the most thorough and competent statistical data bases currently available in the Church of England. This statistical chapter offers a brief introduction to the information made available from the survey. Each participating diocese will subsequently receive a more extended analysis of its own data, and more detailed reports will be developed on aspects of the national scene. The overall value of the project could still be further enhanced by the participation of those churches which have so far not returned their questionnaires.

THE ANALYSIS

7.6   By the end of July 1987, 97 per cent of the returned questionnaires had been prepared for computer analysis. The following statistics are, therefore, computed on the basis of 6,684 churches or worship centres. According to *Church Statistics: some facts and figures about the Church of England* (Church House Publishing, 1984), the 43 dioceses of the Provinces of Canterbury and York, excluding Europe, contain 16,704 churches. The analysis, therefore, represents 40 per cent of these churches.

BAPTISM

7.7   The service for 'the baptism of children' in the *Alternative Service Book 1980* argues that

> Children who are too young to profess the Christian faith are baptised on the understanding that they are brought up as Christians within the family of the church.

In this sense, the Church of England has a particular responsibility to the infants, children and young people who come to Anglican fonts.

7.8   On the one hand, it is true that the secularisation process of the past decades has significantly reduced the number of infants presented for baptism. On the other hand, those who are now presented for baptism may well represent more of a spiritual quest or commitment and less of an accepted social rite of passage.

7.9   The data demonstrates that in 1985 some 217,000 infants, children and young people under the age of 14 were baptised in the Church of England. By their second birthday, nearly one-third (32 per cent) of infants have been baptised in Anglican churches; another 2 per cent have been baptised by their sixth birthday and a further 1 per cent by their fourteenth birthday. Roughly the same proportion of boys and girls are baptised.

7.10   These figures might suggest that the Church of England has accepted pastoral and catechetical responsibility for some 2,881,000 infants, children and young people under the age of 14.

PARENTS AND TODDLERS

7.11   One way in which the Church of England is increasingly demonstrating its commitment to the very young and to their parents is through parent–and–toddler groups. Slightly more than one church in six is now offering this kind of facility, and making contact with around 77,000 children under the age of six, or about 2 per cent of that age group. A slightly higher proportion of girls are brought to church–related parent–and–toddler groups than boys.

7.12   A significant aspect of the work of these groups is among the parents. There are two adults present for every three children. Most of the adults who support these groups are mothers. Generally one father comes to these groups for every 17 or 18 mothers.

PLAYGROUPS

7.13   Playgroups operate for slightly older children than parent-and-toddler groups and require more professional organisation. While one church in six offers parent-and-toddler facilities, less than one in 14 offers some form of playgroup. It is likely that many churches, having initiated playgroups in the sixties, now leave them to the Pre-School Playgroup Association. The playgroups work mainly for 2 to 5 year-olds, although a few younger babies also seem to attend alongside their older brothers and sisters.

7.14   Church-related playgroups are making contact with around 35,000 children under the age of six, or about 1 per cent of that age group. A slightly higher proportion of girls than boys are brought to church-related playgroups. Generally there is one adult involved in the playgroup for every five children.

SUNDAY SCHOOLS

7.15   The Sunday school has become a generic name for the Church's work among children. It is not unusual to hear the Tuesday afternoon activity club referred to as a Sunday school, although it neither resembles school nor takes place on Sunday. More than half (53 per cent) of the churches operate some form of 'Sunday school' activity for children.

7.16   The main age-group attracted by Sunday schools are the 6 to 9 year-olds. Currently Sunday schools make contact with around 132,000 6 to 9 year-olds, or about 6 per cent of that age group.
    A number of Sunday schools begin recruiting significantly before children reach the age of beginning day school. Currently Sunday schools make contact with around 74,000 2 to 5 year-olds, or about 3 per cent of that age group. A number of Sunday schools even welcome babies under the age of two. Currently Sunday schools make contact with around 6,000 infants under the age of 2, or 0.5 per cent of that age group.

7.17   Although Sunday schools tend to lose their members after the age of 9, there are still around 62,000 10 to 13 year-olds in contact with Sunday schools, or about 2.5 per cent of that age group.

7.18   Among the 2 to 5 year-olds, Sunday schools are already recruiting a higher proportion of girls than boys. This imbalance between the sexes becomes more pronounced among the older age-groups. Thus, 55 per cent of the 2 to 5 year-old Sunday school members are girls, and the proportion rises to 58 per cent among the 6 to 9 year-olds and 61 per cent among the 10 to 13 year-olds.

7.19   The data demonstrates that there is one Sunday school teacher or a helper for every six pupils. In practice, this means a body of around 47,000 volunteers concerned with the Church's Sunday school work among 2 to 13 year-olds. About one-third of these volunteers are themselves teenagers. It is much more common for Sunday school teachers and helpers to be female (78 per cent) than male (22 per cent).

CPAS ORGANISATIONS

7.20   The CPAS organisations constitute a kind of national network and framework for work among children and young people through Scramblers, Climbers, Explorers and Pathfinders. About one church in nine claims to be operating CPAS-related schemes. These schemes begin to recruit members during the pre-school years and continue to increase membership into the early teens.

7.21   CPAS-related schemes currently make contact with around 12,000 2 to 5 year-olds (0.5 per cent of that age-group), 23,000 6 to 9 year-olds (1 per cent of that age-group) and 30,000 10 to 13 year-olds (1.3 per cent of that age-group). Like Sunday schools, CPAS-related schemes attract a higher proportion of girls than boys. This means that 54 per cent of the 2 to 5 year-olds are girls and the proportion rises to 55 per cent of the 6 to 9 year-olds and 57 per cent of the 10 to 13 year-olds.

7.22   There are around 10,000 adult leaders involved in CPAS-related schemes. A higher proportion of men are involved in CPAS leadership than in Sunday school leadership: 41 per cent of the leaders in CPAS-related schemes are men.

7.23   If the membership of Sunday school and CPAS groups is aggregated, the data suggests that through these groups the Church of

England has contact with around 87,000 2 to 5 year-olds, or about 4 per cent of that age-group; 155,000 6 to 9 year-olds, or about 7 per cent of that age-group, and 93,000 10 to 13 year-olds, or about 4 per cent of that age-group.

YOUTH CLUBS

7.24 Youth clubs which attract 10 to 13 year-olds are operated by nearly one in every four churches (24 per cent). This kind of youth club provision makes contact with around 46,000 10 to 13 year-olds, or about 2 per cent of that age-group. Slightly more than half (53 per cent) of these young youth club members are girls.

7.25 Many of these groups which call themselves youth clubs also include some under 10 year-olds. They make contact with around 10,000 6 to 9 year-olds, or about 0.4 per cent of that age-group.

CHURCH CHOIRS

7.26 When children leave Sunday school around the age of 9, it is often the church choir which provides their next firm link with the Church. Nearly half (49 per cent) of the churches have choirs which include 10 to 13 year-old girls, while only slightly fewer (47 per cent) include 10 to 13 year-old boys. All told, church choirs make contact with around 31,000 10 to 13 year-olds, or about 1 per cent of that age group. There are approximately four girls of this age group in church choirs for every three boys.

7.27 Many church choirs start recruiting children considerably under the age of 10. There are also around 12,000 6 to 9 year-olds in church choirs, or about 0.5 per cent of that age-group. Among this younger age-group there is an almost identical number of boys (49 per cent) and girls (51 per cent).

7.28 Most of the churches which invite children to join the choir also make arrangements for some kind of choir practice. Nine out of every ten (90 per cent) of the child choristers are also involved in a regular practice, which provides them with another significant point of contact with the Church and may involve some form of instruction.

SERVERS

7.29   Like church choirs, serving provides another traditional point of contact between children or young people and the Church. While many churches now recruit more girls into the church choir than boys, serving remains more of a male preserve. Two out of every five churches (42 per cent) provide opportunities for 10 to 13 year-old boys to act as servers, compared with one in five (22 per cent) which provide similar opportunities for 10 to 13 year-old girls.

7.30   All told, serving makes contact with about 4,000 10 to 13 year-old girls (0.3 per cent of the girls in that age-group) and 7,000 10 to 13 year-old boys (0.5 per cent of the boys in that age-group). A few younger children, less than 2,000, are also involved as servers.

BELL RINGERS

7.31   Some churches which possess a ring of bells make a point of recruiting young ringers. Nearly a third (31 per cent) of the churches involve under 14 year-old boys as ringers, while a quarter (26 per cent) involve girls of this age. The majority of churches which have any young ringers appear to recruit only one or two, often the children of adult ringers. All told, there are a little over 4,000 young people under the age of 14 involved in this aspect of church life.

SCOUTS AND GUIDES

7.32   Brownies, Guides, Cubs and Scouts provide a very significant point of contact between a number of churches and young people. Historically a number of groups were sponsored by churches, and others became identified with a church because they meet in a church hall or because churchgoers play a key role in their leadership. Thus nearly one in five (19 per cent) of churches feel that they have a regular relationship with some aspect of the scouting movement.

7.33   More churches have this kind of contact with Brownies and Guides (18 per cent) than with Cubs and Scouts (12 per cent). More 6 to 9 year-olds than 10 to 13 year-olds are brought into contact with the churches through these organisations. Thus, church-related Cubs and Scouts provide for contact with around 44,000 6 to 9 year-old boys, or about 4 per cent of the boys in that age-group, and around 37,000 10 to 13 year-old boys, or about 3 per cent of the boys in that age-group. At the same time, church-related Brownies and Guides provide contact with around 58,000 6 to 9 year-old girls or about 5 per cent of the girls in that age-group, and around 44,000 10 to 13 year-old girls, or about 4 per cent of the girls in that age-group.

7.34   In addition to these church-related groups, a number of Brownie, Guide, Cub and Scout groups which are not church-related still provide opportunities of church contact for children and young people through attendance at such events as parade services. If these groups are taken into account in addition to those described above, the number of children and young people who are in touch with the churches through Scouting and Guiding organisations is increased considerably. Thus all told, Cubs and Scouts bring around 69,000 6 to 9 year-old boys into church from time to time, or about 6 per cent of the boys in that age-group, and around 60,000 10 to 13 year-old boys, or around 5 per cent of the boys in that age-group. At the same time, Brownies and Guides bring around 102,000 6 to 9 year-old girls to church from time to time, or about 9 per cent of the girls in that age-group, and around 85,000 10 to 13 year-old girls, or about 7 per cent of the girls in that age-group.

CHURCH UNIFORMED GROUPS

7.35   A branch of the Boys' Brigade or Girls' Brigade is present in about one Anglican church in sixty. This group of organisations is much stronger among boys than girls. There are about seven male members for every three female members. Although these groups reach considerably fewer children and young people than the church-related Scouts or Guides, they tend to keep their membership further into the teenage years. All told, through the Boys' Brigade and Girls' Brigade Anglican churches are making contact with about 4,500 6 to 9 year-olds and 4,200 10 to 13 year-olds.

7.36   A branch of the Church Lads' and Church Girls' Brigade is present in about one Anglican church in seventy-five. This organisation does not have quite so many members in Anglican churches as the Boys' Brigade and Girls' Brigade, but has developed a more even spread among boys and girls. There are about seven male members for every six female members. Unlike the other uniformed groups, the Church Lads' and Church Girls' Brigade actually appears to increase its membership into the early teenage years. All told, through the

Church Lads' and Church Girls' Brigade, Anglican churches are making contact with about 2,800 6 to 9 year-olds and 3,000 10 to 13 year-olds.

7.37   A branch of the Girls' Friendly Society is present in about one Anglican church in ninety. All told, through the Girls' Friendly Society, Anglican churches are making contact with about 1,200 6 to 9 year-old girls and 1,200 10 to 13 year-old girls.

OTHER UNIFORMED GROUPS

7.38   In addition to the church-related uniformed groups and the Brownie, Guide, Cub and Scout groups, there is a range of other uniformed groups which bring children and young people into regular contact with the churches through such occasions as parade services. The data demonstrates that these other groups bring around 4,000 6 to 9 year-olds and around 4,000 10 to 13 year-olds into church on a regular basis.

If all the uniformed groups, church-related and non-church-related, are aggregated, they bring the Church of England into contact with around 184,000 6 to 9 year-olds, or about 8 per cent of that age-group, and around 157,000 10 to 13 year-olds, or about 7 per cent of that age-group.

CONFIRMATION

7.39   The preferred age for confirmation varies greatly from place to place within the Church of England. While some places are experimenting with the admission of children and young people to Communion prior to confirmation, others prefer to encourage early confirmation as a gateway to Communion. In 1985, about 30,000 young people were confirmed under the age of 14. This represents nearly two in every five (38 per cent) of the confirmation candidates during that year. Among the under 14 year-olds, seven girls were confirmed for every five boys.

SUNDAY CONTACT

7.40   In addition to the provisions made by the churches specifically for children and young people, a number of under 14 year-olds come into regular contact with the Church through attending all-age services on a Sunday.

Another section of the questionnaire asked churches to make a careful list of all their Sunday services and activities, including crèches, Sunday schools, 'junior church', youth groups and so on. When all this information is aggregated, the data shows the total number of children and young people who have contact with the churches on a normal Sunday.

On a normal Sunday one church in three (34 per cent) has contact with infants under the age of 2; 57 per cent have contact with 2 to 5 year-olds, and nearly two in three (64 per cent) have contact with 6 to 9 year-olds and 10 to 13 year-olds.

All told, on a normal Sunday the Church has contact with 22,000 under 2 year-olds, or 1.8 per cent of that age-group; 76,000 2 to 5 year-olds, or 1.8 per cent of that age-group; 154,000 6 to 9 year-olds, or 6.8 per cent of that age-group, and 141,000 10 to 13 year-olds, or 6 per cent of that age-group.

CONCLUSION

7.41   The baptism statistics have suggested that the Church of England has accepted pastoral and catechetical responsibility for over one-third of the child population, or some 2,881,000 infants, children and young people under the age of 14.

7.42   The other statistics have demonstrated the number of infants, children and young people who are in touch with the Church of England through a variety of organisations and activities. Particular attention has been drawn to the important role of Sunday schools and CPAS-related schemes, to the uniformed organisations and to church choirs and serving. Many more infants, children and young people are in regular contact with the church through attending services with their parents.

NOTE

In computing these statistics we gratefully acknowledge the use of the *1986 Population Estimates for England and Wales* published by the Office of Population Censuses and Surveys (Reference PP1 87/1 and Crown copyright).

Leslie J Francis
David W Lankshear

TABLE 1   RESPONSE RATE BY DIOCESE

Diocese (and *archdeaconry)	Number of worship centres	Number of replies	Response Rate
Bath and Wells	586	453	82%
Birmingham	207	173	84%
Blackburn	293	222	76%
Bristol	210	186	89%
Carlisle	340	266	78%
Chelmsford	576	293	51%
Chester	374	277	74%
Chichester	512	368	72%
Derby	345	206	60%
Durham	309	186	60%
Ely	328	201	61%
Gloucester	408	343	84%
Hereford	403	188	47%
Isle of Wight*	60	49	81%
Lichfield	614	475	77%
London	484	323	67%
Oxford	824	495	60%
Peterborough	374	252	67%
St Albans	397	273	69%
Salisbury	575	412	72%
Sheffield	214	116	54%
Southwell	300	244	81%
Truro	301	250	83%
Worcester	262	245	93%
York	618	425	69%

8. Recommendations

CHAPTER 1

1.   The Church should seriously consider what priority it places on serving the needs of all children in our contemporary society. Parishes, deaneries and dioceses should acknowledge their responsibility
  - to learn from those already involved in social work with children,
  - to investigate particular local pressures on children,
  - to establish practical ways of contributing to children's support and enrichment.

2.   PCCs should carefully consider the suitability of new leaders to whom they delegate responsibility for work with children in the parish.

CHAPTER 2

1.   Parishes, deaneries and dioceses undertaking children's evangelistic missions should examine the appropriate basis for them, with special reference to follow-up work, family involvements and peer group pressures.

2.   The Church, nationally and locally, should actively support the efforts of uniformed groups to evaluate the moral and spiritual aspects of their work with children.

3.   Parishes should consider how they can effectively support the best traditions of Christian marriage and family life, while affirming their active and sensitive concern and care for all for whom this is not a reality.

4. Boards of General Synod should include the consideration of children's needs and experience in their Reports to Synod whenever this is appropriate.

5. The Board of Mission and Unity and the Board of Education should explore as a matter of urgency appropriate ways to enable children and leaders to respond to a multi-ethnic society.

CHAPTER 3

1. PCCs, wherever possible, should plan at least one venture for the coming year in which adults and children are involved together in learning and exploring what it means to be followers 'in the Way', and should develop a continuing pattern for learning together.

2. Diocesan Education Officers (for adult, youth and children's work) should actively explore and implement ways of creating joint learning experiences for children and adults.

CHAPTER 4

1. The Board of Education should commission an appraisal of the research into faith development and its implications for Christian nurture. Further research is required into the critical stages of transition and growth in a child's spiritual development, and the appropriate support to be offered by the Church to parents and children at these times.

2. A resolution of the issue of Communion before Confirmation is required as a matter of urgency.

3. The Board of Education and the Liturgical Commission should examine the need for new liturgies to serve all-age worship, and in particular for a form of Eucharist suitable for when children are present. There should be full consultation with leaders and parents of young children.

4. Funding should be sought for a field officer, responsible to the Board of Education, to promote experiments, produce resources and disseminate information relating to all-age learning.

CHAPTER 5

1.   Parishes should review the support they offer to those who lead their educational work, with particular reference to
   - realistic finance for resources,
   - regular training,
   - personal support and development.

2.   Those responsible for ministerial training should review the adequacy of their consideration of children in the Church and society. The possibility of liaison with professionals in teacher training departments in universities and in higher and further education colleges should be considered.

3.   The training of leaders for all-age learning should be explored by Diocesan Education Committees in conjunction with the recommendations about developing leadership in *Faith in the City* and the guidelines suggested in *Called to be Adult Disciples*.

4.   Diocesan Education Councils should reassess their staff and resources in the light of the training and assistance which will need to be offered to parishes to implement the Recommendations in this Report.

Appendix 1   Discussion Questions

In a lengthy report, it is not easy to highlight the practical steps a parish might take in response to our conclusions. We have suggested at a number of points that parishes (or deaneries) might find it helpful to review the place of children in their total life in the light of the report. This appendix provides some of the questions a parish might find helpful in tackling such a review. We hope that the most appropriate questions will be selected to meet the situation in a particular parish. For convenience they are grouped under three major headings: assessing the situation, identifying objectives and developing resources. It would be tedious to repeat at length the ideas associated with each question but it is important to stress that the questions are only comprehensible in the light of the extended argument in the earlier chapters.

We suggest also that parishes use a variety of methods in tackling the questions. For example, a preliminary fact-finding exercise might be undertaken by a few members, the meeting might be divided into smaller groups to discuss particular aspects of the Report, a diocesan officer might be invited to assist the discussion, and above all the video presentation available from the Board of Education might be used to start the discussion.

ASSESSING THE SITUATION

It is essential to remember just how strongly coloured by our own experience is our impression of childhood today. This is as much true if we are married and have our own families as if we are single. It is surprisingly also true for those of our congregation who have young families and are themselves comparatively young. The pressures and opportunities of childhood identified in the first chapter are signifi-

93

cantly different today even from those experienced by people who are now only a few years removed from them. This makes the task of assessing the situation for today's children - especially those with no Christian or Church connections - particularly important.

1. How do we find out what it is like to be a child living in this parish in 1988?

2. What 'good news' do the children in this area need? What do they hear?

3. What opportunities to listen to children are made by our church?

4. How many children are in contact in some way with the Church? What are their needs?

5. What are the needs of children and families in our area who are outside the Church?

6. What resources do we have to meet these needs and either to build on these contacts or to make contact?

IDENTIFYING OBJECTIVES

We have tried throughout the report to keep a balance between the ideal we uphold and the practical realities of parish life. It is important in setting objectives in this context to try and preserve the same balance. It is unlikely that you will revolutionise your work with children either within the Church or within the wider community, but comparatively small changes of priority, attitude and practice may produce very significant changes for the place of children in the life of your parish.

1. Which of the models described in chapter 3 most influences our work with children?

2. What opportunities are there for different age groups to work and worship with each other? How do our activities as a parish enable children and adults to learn and grow together in knowledge, Christian experience and worship; exploring, celebrating and living out the Christian story?

3. Which activities in our church are appropriate for particular age groups?

4. How far does our worship and teaching provide for the different stages of faith? Do the descriptions of stages by John Westerhoff echo our experience and the experience of people we know?

5. How do we help members of all ages to grow in spiritual awareness?

6. What does our church mean by family worship? Check out what different members of the congregation think it implies.

7. How far do the children and adults share in the worldwide mission of the Church, and meet with Christians of other Churches?

DEVELOPING RESOURCES

The same cautionary note applies to this section. It is easy to be angered by the implication that appropriately qualified leaders are readily available in every parish. We recognise that this is not the reality but would suggest that the pattern of learning we have described might attract those who otherwise would feel that they had nothing to offer in this context. It is clearly essential that parishes accept the need to match expectations they make of leaders with the appropriate resources and support.

1. Identify the different kinds of leadership in our church. Who exercises them?

2. What opportunities are there for children to take the lead?

3. What contribution do or could families make to our church?

4. What opportunities are given for leaders to grow in personal faith and in leadership skills?

5. How does the parish help its leaders to grow in confidence, and how do we encourage new leaders to arise? What support do we provide or discover for them? What resources are available to them?

6. How far do we need to co-operate with other parishes and denominations in our work for and with children and parents?

7. What help can we obtain from the diocese and other agencies to support our leaders?

Appendix 2 Booklist

The Child in the Church, Reports of the Working Parties on 'The Child in the Church' and 'Understanding Christian Nurture' (British Council of Churches)

Child Development made Simple, Richard Lansdown (Heinemann)

Child Development, Geoffrey Brown (Open Books)

Children in Danger, A Factfile about children today, 1987 edition (National Children's Home)

Children at Risk, David Porter (Kingsway Publications)

Preventing Child Sexual Assault, Michelle Elliott (Bedford Square Press)

Twenty Questions and Answers about Child Abuse, John Bradford (Church of England Children's Society)

The Rise and Fall of the Sunday School Movement in England 1780-1980, Philip B Cliff (National Christian Education Council)

Centuries of Childhood, Philippe Aries (Penguin)

Jesus and the Children, Hans-Ruedi Weber (World Council of Churches)

Will Our Children Have Faith?, John H Westerhoff III (Seabury Press, USA)

A Pilgrim People: Learning through the Christian Year, John H Westerhoff III (Seabury Press, USA)

Stages of Faith, James Fowler (Harper and Row)

Becoming Adult, Becoming Christian, James Fowler (Harper and Row) (This includes a useful summary of the stages in chapter 3.)

What Prevents Christian Adults from Learning?, John Hull (SCM Press)

Our Faith Story, A Patrick Purnell SJ (Collins)

Guidelines, Jim Gallagher (Collins)

Learning Community, John Sutcliffe (Denholm House Press)

Bringing up Children in the Christian Faith, John H Westerhoff III (Winston Press, USA)

Onward Christian Parents, Terence Copley (Church House Publishing)

What Can a Parent Do?, Micki and Terri Quinn (Veritas)

Understanding Children, Maggie Durran (Marshall Pickering)

The Price of Love, Jane Davies (Mowbrays)

Parents Talking Television, Comedia Series No 46, edited by Philip Simpson (Comedia Publishing Group)

Video Violence and Children, edited by Geoffrey Barlow and Alison Hill (Hodder and Stoughton)

Exploring Inner Space, David Hay (Penguin)

Helping Children to Pray, Ruth Cardwell (The Grail)

The Bible, A Child's Playground, Roger and Gertrude Gobbel (SCM Press)

The Original Vision, Edward Robinson (Religious Experience Research Unit)

Communion before Confirmation?, (Church House Publishing)

All Generations, A Handbook for Leaders of Family Worship. The Offchurch Group (Church House Publishing)

Once Upon a Group, Michael Kindred (Michael Kindred, 20 Dover Street, Southwell, Notts, NG25 0EZ)

A video to promote discussion of some of the issues in the Report is available from The National Society, Church House, Great Smith Street, London SW1P 3NZ. Also called *Children in the Way,* the video is scripted and presented by Nigel Forde, the well-known broadcaster and member of the Riding Lights theatre company. A discussion leaflet is included in each pack. The video costs £12 plus 65p postage, and is available *on direct retail sale only,* not through bookshops. Cheques for the video should be made payable to 'The National Society'.